THE ADVENTURES OF PAR-MAN

VOLUME ONE

A NEVER-ENDING QUEST FOR GOLF NIRVANA

BY E.J. ROBB

"The Adventures of Par-Man, Volume I: A Never-Ending Quest for Golf Nirvana," by E.J. Robb. ISBN 978-1-62137-941-6 (softcover), 978-1-62137-942-3 (eBook).

Published 2016 by Virtualbookworm.com Publishing Inc., P.O. Box 9949, College Station, TX, 77842, US.

©2016 E.J. Robb. All rights reserved. No part of this publication may be reproduced, stored in a retrieval system, or transmitted in any form or by any means, electronic, mechanical, recording or otherwise, without the prior written permission of E.J. Robb.

DEDICATION

This book is dedicated to the hundreds of golfers in Kansas and Missouri who put up with me joining their groups over the last twenty-five years. You were all wonderful, especially the OP Saturday morning group that, after playing with them a few times as a single, invited me to join their band of Merry Men.

A special dedication to Tom Bartoszewski who passed away Aug. 15, 2016. Par-Man had the honor of playing the last round of golf Bob was able to enjoy before going to the great fairway in the sky.

Thanks to Larry, Mike, Tom R., Dan W., Dan Y., Jon, Chuck, George, Brian E., Jimmy, Bill, Brad H., Jim, Kurt, and Tom S. You guys make every Saturday morning something to look forward to.

A special thanks to Earl and Terry, marshals at OP.

Acknowledgements

Listed in order of appearance so there is no favoritism.

Golf Digest
Golf Handicap and Information Network (GHIN)
Sykes-Lady Golf Course, Overland Park, Kansas
Prairie Highlands Golf Course, Olathe, Kansas
Kansas University Hospital
Painted Hills Golf Course, Kansas City, Kansas
Falcon Lakes, Basehor, Kansas
Tiffany Greens, Kansas City, Missouri
Sunflower Hills Golf Course, Bonner Springs, Kansas
Tomahawk Golf Course, Shawnee, Kansas
St. Andrews Golf Course, Overland Park, Kansas
Heritage Golf Course, Olathe, Kansas
Minor Golf Course, Kansas City, Missouri
Dan Pohl PGA Professional
The National, a Tom Watson course in Kansas City, Missouri
Canyon Farms Golf Club, Lenexa, Kansas
Shadow Glen, Olathe, Kansas
Deer Creek Golf Course, Overland Park, Kansas
Falcon Ridge Golf Course, Lenexa, Kansas
Swope Memorial Golf Course, Kansas City, Missouri
Shawnee Golf and Country Club, Shawnee, Kansas

OTHER E. J. ROBB BOOKS

The Adventures of Par-Man Volume One
The Adventures of Par-Man Volume Two (April 2017)
The Adventures of Par-Man Volume Three (August 2017)

The **Richard Steele** Series
Steele Trap, released 2015
Steele Away, released 2015
Steele Armor, released 2016

To be released
Steele Valor, (to be released in 2017)
Steele Judgement
Heart of Steele
Hard as Steele
Power of Steele
Knight of Steele
Days of Steele

The new Science Fiction thriller, *The Creation of God,* will be released in 2017

Prologue

Keep in mind, according to Golf Digest who surveyed data from the Golf Handicap and Information Network (GHIN), most Saturday golfers have a handicap right about bogey golf. **[50% of all golfers will never be able to brag of having a handicap under 18.]**

Even though the average score for all amateur golfers is slightly over 100 the handicaps are much lower. Handicaps are a measure of what your potential is, not what you generally shoot. In 1991 men had an average handicap of 16.3 and in 2013 it had dropped to 14.3. Women were somewhat higher at 28.9 and 26.5 respectively. The reason for the big difference between the average score and average handicap is, as was just mentioned, a handicap is an indication of what you are capable of shooting, not what you usually *actually* shoot.

Because a handicap uses the ten best out of the last twenty scores the handicap is a lagging indicator if your game is deteriorating and a leading indicator if your game is improving. In other words handicaps drop quickly and rise slowly. A few interesting averages to consider:

	MEN	WOMEN
Average driver distance	200-240 yards	160-210 yards
Average 6 iron	130-160 yards	70-130 yards
Pitching Wedge	80-120 yards	50-80 yards

When asked how far they hit their drives men tend to overestimate by 18-35 yards and women underestimate by 10-15 yards. If you want to achieve nirvana, a round of par or better, then the following are your target numbers: 1) you need to hit 12 of 18 greens, 2) about 14 fairways, 3) have 7 one putts per round, 4) have 11 pars and finally 5) at least one birdie for every 18 holes.

If you are a scratch golfer or better then you might want to put this book back on the shelf. You won't understand what we weekend golfers go through on a regular basis. This book is about the exploits of Par-Man, a kind of Super Hero, whose mission is to help the average golfer achieve one round at even par or better before they need to make tee times with the Great Starter in the sky.

Par-Man does this not by giving golf lessons, improving mechanics or even better equipment. No, with special super powers, he accomplishes his noble mission of helping each golfer, one by one, learn to relax and build confidence toward that one exceptional round of golf. Par-Man is not a trained psychologist or skilled in philosophy. His super power comes from his ability to use levity to get his golfing associates to relax and play with confidence. It works, sometimes. Par-Man has had actually helped some of his playing partners achieve the ultimate goal, par or better for eighteen holes.

While you, the reader, may not consider humor a super power then you don't know how hard it is to smile after three putting from four feet or hitting your driver as far as your wedge. Smiling or helping others smile after that takes a super power.

Par-Man was taught the importance of relaxing while golfing by taking his eight year old granddaughter on a shopping trip. At the end of this short story the golf connection will be obvious. The story of that shopping trip went something like this:

> In the last three months I have been able to spend many hours of quality time with my youngest granddaughter. In that short amount of time she has taught me several things. About two months ago I learned that amazing shopping opportunities existed just a few blocks from our house.
>
> It was a rainy Saturday so there was no golf in my immediate future and Sophie, my granddaughter, was bored sitting at home. She walked into the TV room and asked, "Grandpa, can we go shopping?"
>
> "What do you need to go shopping for?"
>
> "I won't know until I get there." She looked at me like I was as dumb as a rock. *The first thing I learned was, don't ask stupid questions.*

"Gee, it's raining and traffic will be a mess and besides as soon as the weather clears I want to go golfing." I really just didn't want to go shopping.

After giving it some thought she said, "Let's go to the 7/Eleven. It's close and we can come back whenever you want."

All of my objections had just been neutralized. What could I say? "Sure, we can do that." *The second thing I learned was arguing with an eight year old was harder than I thought.*

The 7/Eleven is less than two minutes away but that was enough time for Sophie to convince me that she should have at least five dollars to spend. And that wasn't really enough. We spent about thirty minutes shopping. Turns out if you don't look at it like you're in a 7/Eleven but a shopping adventure you can have as much fun as you want. She carefully spent her money so she could get something for grandma and mommy. *The third thing I learned was not to expect anything to be given to you if you can get it yourself.*

When I asked her what she was getting me I got the 'dumb as a rock' look again. "You're right here. Get whatever you want." *The fourth thing I learned was that I hadn't learned the first thing.*

As she shopped and repeatedly asked the clerk how much something cost I noticed the other patrons would smile. She must have brought a little happiness to a dozen people in that half hour. I found that I was enjoying myself, shopping at the 7/Eleven. *The fifth thing I learned was that she made more people smile in thirty minutes than I had in the last three days.*

When we were done and headed home Sophie asked, "Why don't we do that again. That was fun."

"You're right. We will do it again."

"She looked at me, smiled, and said, "I love it when you give me money." Then she reached up from the back seat and hugged my neck. *The sixth thing I learned was that contrary to conventional wisdom money can buy happiness.*

After the purchases had been distributed to mommy and grandma the weather cleared and I went out golfing. I was replaying the shopping trip in my mind and smiled as the memories came back to me. I played a pretty good round of golf. At the sixteenth hole I was only six over par and had two birdies. *The seventh thing I learned was that golf really is a mental game and a good attitude helps your score.*

Unfortunately I finished twelve over par. *The last thing I learned is that there is also some skill necessary to really golf well.* (Reprinted by permission, *Hot Air News,* 2016)

What follows in this book is absolutely, well mostly, true. The names have been changed to protect the innocent and the guilty. Well, except one and that's Adam. I did not change his name because he was such a jackass I wanted him to realize when he reads this book that he had been given the honor of playing a round of golf with Par-Man, and didn't appreciate it. You, the reader, will know what I mean when you get to the sixth hole.

For the last twenty plus years Par-Man has been preparing for his secret mission. Always going out as a single he relied on no-shows and the kindness of others to get to play golf. They are always out there, the no-shows. It's too late, my wife won't let me, it just finished raining, the course will be too wet, it's too hot, and my personal favorite, I haven't been playing well lately. (I'm sure you'll get better sitting on the couch watching Jim Furyk shoot a record 58 at the Travelers.) All of these and many more have allowed me to meet literally hundreds of wonderful men, women and even some kids.

The structure of this book is simple. There are eighteen holes instead of chapters. And yes, we will make the turn and there is a nineteenth hole. Each hole starts with a little tip on proper golf etiquette and ends with, well, you'll see.

This cobbled together round of eighteen holes covers many different courses and about fifteen years. There are eighteen holes and most are at different courses and pick-up the round in progress. Some background will be provided but you, the reader, need to use your understanding of the game of golf to pick-up the action at each hole.

The sole purpose of this book is to entertain, enlighten and inform. Hopefully when you are asked to let a single golfer join your group you will welcome him or her. Just like you, they are striving to celebrate the day they finally have a scorecard that is at par or better. **[In 1962 Jack Nicklaus, got his first PGA tour check at the L. A. Open. He shot par and collected $33.33]**

Did you know that during WW II the Augusta National Golf Club was closed and used to raise cattle for the war effort?

Contents

The Front Nine
HOLE ONE: The Starter 1
HOLE TWO: Friends 9
HOLE THREE: The Nemesis 15
HOLE FOUR: The Teacher 21
HOLE FIVE: Doctor, Please 26
HOLE SIX: Adam 31
HOLE SEVEN: The Champion 36
HOLE EIGHT: Oh, God 41
HOLE NINE: The Rider 46
THE TURN: 51

The Back Nine
HOLE TEN: Celia 54
HOLE ELEVEN: The Pro 59
HOLE TWELVE: The Gambler 64
HOLE THIRTEEN: The Resident 69
HOLE FOURTEEN: The Old Man 73
HOLE FIFTEEN: The Shot 78
HOLE SIXTEEN: The Fiver 83
HOLE SEVENTEEN: The Strategist 88
HOLE EIGHTEEN: The International 93
HOLE NINETEEN: 97

The Front Nine

HOLE ONE
THE STARTER

Proper golf etiquette starts on the first hole when you meet your playing partners. They will form their impression of you in the first ten seconds. Be polite and respectful. Make it a good impression; there will be plenty of time for them to learn otherwise. Remember, it is better to keep quiet and have others think you a fool than speak and remove all doubt.

AS I DROVE INTO THE PARKING LOT of the Overland Park Sykes-Lady Golf course I knew I was in trouble, big trouble. It was packed. In early spring, April to be exact, Kansas can have some spectacular days. This was one of them. It had been predicted two days earlier by our usually unreliable weather forecasters and every golfer in the area had called for a tee time. To make matters worse it was a Saturday. I had originally planned to work but at the last minute the golf gods decided to put me to the test. The plant cancelled the extra overtime and I was free to pursue, again, the quest of playing eighteen holes at even par, or better.

I exited the car, walked quickly to the clubhouse, so no other single golfer would get ahead of me, and asked the question. "Have you got an open tee time for one?"

"No, not really. We're packed for the next several hours. You know with the nice weather and all." Sean knew me and sympathized with my plight. He knew I was here because this course, to the chagrin of some, allowed fivesomes.

Since most people golf in foursomes I had a better chance here as a walk-on. "Here's what I'll do. I'll sell you eighteen holes and you go see the starter. He'll work you in if he can."

I knew my chances were slim but there were no other options. "Thanks, Sean. That will be fine." If things didn't work out I knew I could get a rain check.

The routine was the same every time. Go see the starter first. So I walked up to the starter, a volunteer sitting in the cart out in the nice weather, and explain my situation. I'm lucky today. I recognize the starter but can't recall his name. "Hi, I'm a single and..."

"Yeah, Sean called down. I don't have anything right now." The starter showed me the iPad he was holding. The course had gone high tech. I could see that for the next three tee times there were five players and they are all checked in. I could also tell that the following four tee times have five scheduled but they were all not at the course yet. There were a couple of blanks on the iPad, a glimmer of hope. **[Nobody knows for sure why the typical golf group became four. Likely it was because setting teams was easier. Fortunately for me this course allows five to a group.]**

"It looks like I have some time to kill so I'll get some balls and be at the driving range. If something opens up let me know."

"I can't leave here. You need to check back in twenty minutes or so."

I made my way back to my car and retrieved my clubs, shoes and paid a visit to the range. I had decided to walk today. The course rents pull carts and I rented one. After hitting a few balls to loosen up I went back to the starters cart still parked at the tee box on the first hole.

"Anything yet?"

"No. Stay close in case."

"I'm going to practice putting for a while."

"Got it."

The practice putting green, or clock, is directly behind the starter near the refreshments. Here most golfers work on chips and short putts and then when the eighteen holes are finished they can work on the chip dip and short shots. It will be easy for the starter to find me if he needs to. I finish putting and sit down to contemplate the upcoming round and how I got into this silly sport. I think about my dad who taught my brother and me to golf.

"It's called golf because all the other four letter words were taken." My dad almost never swore but if he had it would have happened on the golf course. There are those that believe the word is actually an acronym for 'Gentlemen Only Ladies Forbidden.'

I know that's not true. King James II, in the mid-1400's, forbade the use of 'ye golf,' Scottish for 'the club.' It seems that the military was letting archery practice suffer in favor of using the clubs out on the links. That's the generally accepted story on where the name 'golf' came from, but hey, who really knows? **[Some believe that the Dutch word 'kolf' meaning club was bastardized by the Scotsmen.]**

My reverie is interrupted. "E. J., hey E. J., I have an opening." It's the starter, the controller of my fate.

I pick up my putter and truck on down to see the starter, pulling my cart behind me. "What time?"

"Right now." The starter points at four men on the tee box. "Join them."

To those not familiar with being a walk-on the starters words have real power. "The starter says I am to join your group." Nine words that carry real power. No one questions the starter; he is the lord of the links.

All four turned, smiled and started introducing themselves. "Hi, I'm Bill."

"E. J."

"I'm Joe."

"E. J."

"Nice to meet you E. J., my name is Ralph. That's Howard." Howard waved. He was busy fishing a ball or tee from his bag.

Now, if I don't remember those names, I have to rely the other three as they talk to their partners. That's why, after embarrassing myself when I couldn't remember a player's name, I developed a method for being able to recall almost any name. It's a technique I'm very proud of.

As soon as one of my new group introduces themselves I play an association game. When Bill said his name I immediately looked at the bill of his cap. It was white so he became Billy Blanco (blanco is Spanish for white-clever, huh.). Joe's name, actually his rather large nose, made me think of Jo-Jo the clown. And Ralph's wardrobe, the checkered pants, made me want to puke, get it, ralph. Howard was the easiest to remember because he was one large man and reminded me of Frank Howard, the slugger for the Washington Senators and later the Detroit Tigers. Yes, I'm old enough to remember the Senators.

This is just a way to remember names. Each of them were extremely cordial and polite as we prepared to tee-off. This group had lost their fifth. They didn't know why, he just was MIA. His misfortune was my good fortune.

Even though I had to wait for a while it was still early. On the first hole the sun was right in our eyes. Protocol demands that everyone stand behind whoever is teeing off and watch where the ball goes. Balls hit directly into the bright sunshine are hard to see and we all want to help each other have that one round that we can brag on forever.

"We usually play a little game. It helps keep the round interesting. You want in?" It was, who the hell was it, asking me a question. Shit, it wasn't the big guy Howard. It wasn't the guy with the clown nose, oh yeah, Joe. It was one of the other two. Hey, I never said the system was perfect. It takes a few holes to get it committed to memory.

"Yeah, sure." Then the light bulb went on. "Uh, what game?"

Same guy whose name I can't remember explained it to me. "We all put in five bucks and play Wolf. Do you know that game?"

"I do." Actually I wasn't sure I did but I didn't want to look stupid. It's a common golf game but since I played as a single I wasn't all that familiar with the rules.

"Good. Let's see what the tee off order is going to be." Standing around in a loose circle the guy who asked me to join in the game, the guy who looked like the leader of this group, the guy whose name I still couldn't remember, threw a tee in the air. Whoever it pointed at would then leave the circle. This process continued until only one was left. You then tee-off in the reverse order. And that order stayed intact for every hole. Whoever had honors was not important any longer.

I was lucky. I was right in the middle and these guys were playing a reasonable game. Five bucks wasn't going to break me. Believe me it could have been a lot worse.

I remember the time last year when I thought that things were going to be worse. Not for me but for a grandfather, in his eighties, who was with his grandson, who was in his early twenties.

I had seen them at the range. The kid could mash the ball and grandpa was one of those that hits it 150 yards straight and then relies on his short game. On the tee box grandpa was being goaded in to an unfair match.

"C'mon grandpa. You get to tee off at the golds and I'll play the tips. I'll give you one stroke per hole."

"That's not fair. You know that you can easily beat me."

"Not so. You've beaten me before."

"On one hole. Never for a full round."

"Let's play for a dollar a hole."

"No."

"Aw, c'mon. We don't get to play that often. Let's make it interesting." The kid was pleading. If he needed the money that bad I was tempted to give it to him just to have him leave the old man alone. The good-natured banter went on for another couple of minutes. Finally grandpa relented.

"Okay, but on every hole I get pick up the ball and throw it and it doesn't count as a stroke against me."

The kid thought a minute and agreed. We all teed off and as expected the kid hit it nearly 300 yards and gramps hit it 160 yards or so. We all played to the green and grandpa never took advantage of his free toss. Had he forgotten?

We all reached the green and the kid was on in three, it was a par five, and his grandfather had taken five, just to reach the green. The old man was twenty feet from the pin and his grandson about fifteen.

"I'm going to take my free throw." He walked toward his ball and then past it. He bent down at the kids ball, picked it up and before anyone could say anything he tossed his grandsons ball into the creek

twenty yards to the side of the green. Before anybody could tell him he had picked up the wrong ball he walked over to his sons' son and said, "I never said I would throw my ball." Then looking at his grandson like a coyote looks at a lamb asked, "Want to make it five bucks a hole."

The rest of us killed ourselves laughing. To junior's credit he took it like a man. Grandpa looked at me and said, "At eighteen bucks that's a cheap lesson." He winked and we all enjoyed the rest of the round.

We were up and the tee-off order was set. We all got off the tee fairly well. I did alright but was feeling my concentration being diverted to the five bucks I might lose. That was counterproductive to shooting my first round ever at par. I knew what to do.

"Howard, here's my money. At the end you can let me know if I have anything coming back."

"Bill keeps score." Howard replied. "It's too complicated for the rest of us."

That was his name. Of course Bronco Billy, no wait, Billy Blanco. As I said, the system takes some getting used to. I gave Bill my money even though he said they trusted me and didn't seem to want it. "Please, then I don't have to remember later."

If I'm going to help others shoot the perfect round then I, Par-Man, have to be able to focus. What's his name, oh yeah, Bill, helped by accepting my donation.

Not much happened until I got to the green. My drive was in the fairway and so was my second shot. My third was pulled left and long. Oh well, a chip and a putt and I'd be sitting pretty. The others were scattered about but three of the four were on in regulation. Ralph, see the system works, took five to get on.

"Howard, you're away." Bill was surveying the green.

Tradition mandates the one furthest from the hole go first. That applies in the fairway and on the green. **[The longest verified putt was at St. Andrews in Scotland, 375 feet]**

""Ralph still isn't on." Joe was pointing at a ball on the fringe.

"Sorry, Ralph."

Now Howard was, in fact, furthest from the flag but Ralph was on the fringe so he could leave the pin in if he so desired. The reason Ralph was going first was convenience. Once Ralph was on they could pull the flag and wouldn't have to take it in and out. No one cared and it isn't Par-Man's mission to be the rules police. People like that are often despised. A good super-hero knows when to keep his mouth shut.

As I waited for Ralph to chip up and on I was reminded of an incident involving two brothers and the rules.

As I recalled the first brother, I don't remember either name. It was before I invented my memory system. He hit a very nice shot into the green. The other brother asked what he had hit.

"A seven."

"That means I can hit an eight." There was some brotherly competition going on.

They both parred the hole and I was pleased to have helped these two start their round and still have hope for the perfect round.

"What did you get?"

"What do you mean? I parred it just like you."

"No, I didn't par it."

"What?" Sheer befuddlement, the one brother was confused and so was I.

"It was a two stroke penalty when I asked you what club you hit. It was a two stroke penalty for you when you answered. I'm assessing myself the penalty. If you want to cheat that's fine by me but our bet is off." The brother doing the talking was smiling.

"That's bullshit and you know it. Put down par for both of us."

"Okay, but don't complain if I ignore some of the other rules."

As the brother who wanted to assess the penalty shots walked off the green he looked at me and winked. "I've got him."

Before we move on to the second hole and a new group I should let you know I lost my five bucks, as expected. None of us had the perfect round but we did have fun. There were some pars and birdies. I even had a birdie, but I needed several more. Turned out

Bill, the keeper of my five dollars won. I was pretty sure my two double bogies didn't help my cause. No one got mad, including me, even when I three putted from six feet. I turned birdie into bogey. My dad told me one time after I threw a club in anger, "Son, you're not good enough to get mad." He was right then and he's still right.

I learned a couple of things from my partners on the very first hole. Ralph ended up with a birdie and an eagle. It sounded better that saying 'double bogey.' (Birdie on a par five is four and an eagle on a par five is three. Four plus three equals seven, that's two over par, or a double bogey, on a par five.) **[Ask your playing partners next time if 'condor' is a real golf term. It is. It's a hole in one on a par five. There are only four that have ever been recorded.]**

I also learned what a South American putt was. It just needed one more revolution to go in. Get the clever reference, one more revolution? Bill also had to let Joe know that no putt is going to be a gimme if you're still away.

There are a couple of real rules that most golfers don't follow. If you're in the woods or rough and during your practice swing knock a leaf off a tree it is a one stroke penalty.

Also in 2008 it became permissible to ask anyone questions about distance. Club selection is still a no-no.

Reason one that golf is better than sex:
A total stranger can be a partner and no one thinks twice about it.

HOLE TWO
Friends

Proper golf etiquette says that you give the others in your group the option of disclosing their handicaps if they so desire. Asking someone you just met what their handicap is would be akin to asking a woman her age. Similarly allow each player the opportunity to disclose any physical limitations they may have. This will save you some embarrassing moments.

FOR OUR SECOND HOLE we travel to Prairie Highlands, still in Kansas-Olathe, Kansas to be exact. Again I showed up as a single and was put with one guy and two women. The point to picking this particular second hole is to show how we can let our preconceived notions affect our ability to enjoy a day with some new friends. If we don't relax and enjoy the day it will be impossible to achieve the goal of golf perfection, a round at par.

The first hole had been a disaster. The women, Julie and Ann, took lots of strokes. Ann took most of them. Julie wasn't really all that bad. The guy, Herb, was actually worse. While waiting to tee off on the first tee box I found out that they were all from Denver. All three had rented their clubs, generally a sure sign that this was going to be a long day.

I was really dreading the next seventeen holes. Par-Man's quest for perfection started with a par on hole one and was hoping for a par on the next hole. The second hole at Prairie Highlands is a short par four up a small hill. There were no hazards, except the three people I was with. Or so I thought.

"Well it looks like we will be waiting." Herb was talking to me. I knew he was talking to me because the two ladies were deep in conversation in the other cart. They seemed oblivious to what was going on ahead of them.

I responded. "It's the first nice day we've had in a while so everybody and his brother is out." It was Sunday and I had just come from Mass, there was no point in complaining, it wouldn't change a thing. "Are you here on vacation or visiting friends?"

"Oh, nothing like that. We are here for support. Julie asked Ann and me to come along with her in case there are any problems." Herb's statement made no sense to me.

"What kind of problems?"

Herb was uncomfortable and clearly regretted his last remark. I looked away and wasn't going to press it. There was a moment of strained silence, broken when Herb said, "Julie played in college and wanted to get out one more time before her surgery tomorrow."

"Nothing serious, I hope." I felt awkward. I felt sorry for the lady but I was feeling good and believed I was looking at a great shot at my goal of perfection. Yeah, I know it had only been one hole but I'm an eternal optimist.

Herb had that look. That look that told me it was very serious. I didn't want a depressing discussion but knew the polite thing to do was ask about her welfare. He must have sensed my apprehension so he volunteered an answer instead of making me ask an uncomfortable question.

"We came here because KU was recommended by the experts in Denver. They have the best treatment center anywhere near us."

That was true; the University of Kansas Hospital is world famous for treatment of many things. My wife had brain surgery there that was unbelievably successful.

Herb continued. "Julie has colon cancer and is having a large section of her intestines removed. She will then undergo radiation treatment. She isn't married and her mother can't travel."

"Are you related?"

"No. we're her next door neighbors."

Those words struck a chord. A couple of years ago I was put with a group that included a grandfather and his grandson. Not too unusual you say. Well consider this; grandpa was paralyzed from the waist down. But he still golfed.

I had never seen a golf cart like the one he had. There was a chair for gramps to sit on. His legs were strapped in place at the shins and waist. The cart steered from the rear, like a forklift truck, and that allowed him to maneuver it up to the ball. Once in position the seat rotated to the rear of the cart and using hydraulics elevated him to a vertical position. Grandpa could now swing. It was all arms of course but none the less he could put a charge into the ball.

Putting was the problem. That's where the grandson came into the picture. Once on the green the kid would putt. They played as a team. I never saw anyone enjoy the game more than those two. I asked the junior member of the partnership how long they had been at it.

"Grandpa has been golfing for about fifty years and has been paralyzed for the last five years. I have been his putter the whole time. He broke his back in a fall."

"Why don't you tee-off and play as well. You could putt for the two of you. No one would care."

Leaning in close he looked at me strangely. "I know that." Then he scrunched up his nose and continued. "But the truth is I really hate golf." Then he smiled and put his index finger to his lips. I nodded. It would be our secret.

I didn't shoot par that day but I felt like a super hero anyhow. I had been a part, a small part, of something special and that was my mission after all.

My look said it all. "Her neighbors?"

"She takes care of her mother. Her mother has lived next door to us for twenty five years. There was no way we could refuse her request." Herb grinned and prepared to tee off. He had no idea that the person with the lower score has honors. I wasn't going to correct him. **[The concept of the low score teeing off first on the next hole traces back over 500 years, to the beginning of golf. The low score was an honor, hence the term 'you have honors.']**

But that's not the end of this hole.

We all hit and Julie found the fairway as did I. As our carts stopped and we waited for the group ahead of us to vacate the green I walked over to speak with her. "Nice shot."

"Better than my first tee shot. I was a little nervous. I haven't played for a while." She was relieved to be in the fairway and happy to be with her friends.

"What college did you play for?"

"Ohio State."

"Oh yeah. I'm from Cleveland originally."

"A Buckeye."

"Well, not really. My dad went to Michigan and I grew up hating Ohio State." There was no need for me to say that. It just sort of popped out.

Julie smiled. "I understand. The Michigan/Ohio State rivalry is really intense."

The group ahead cleared the green and Ann was away. She hit the ball off the toe of her club and it went sideways into the native grass. That's what we call an area that doesn't get mowed. We all went over to look but it was lost. Ann looked at her friend and asked, "How do I count that?"

Julie looked at her and spoke. "You don't. It's just barely lost. If we took the time to do a thorough search we would find it. Just drop one and hit again."

That's when I was introduced to the concept of a 'barely lost' ball. What a gracious way to bail someone out. Ann didn't care. Par-Man was not going to be able to help her achieve the par plateau. None of them were going to reach that level today. But a good super hero never quits and I was a good super hero.

I said, "Yeah, just put it here in the fairway and you're hitting two." Par-Man was determined to help.

Ann looked at me quizzically. "Hitting to what?"

Julie laughed and Ann just shrugged.

I didn't keep track of anybody's strokes but my own. I was on in two and only about fifteen feet away. A birdie would sure help. **[Birdie was a term coined by American Ab Smith who initially referred** to it as a 'bird of a shot.']It would give me an insurance stroke. I suspected I would need it with sixteen holes to go. In my quest for the par round I have started well several times only to end up coming up short of my goal. Once I was at even par through the first nine holes, then the bottom fell out. So if I could get minus one with sixteen holes to go, well that would be a plus.

When it was my turn I took some extra time looking at the break. There wasn't much break but a little at the end. As I stood over the ball I heard, "What's he waiting for?"

It was Ann talking to Julie. Julie responded, "He's trying to figure out that little break at the end. It looks subtle but in fact the ball will move quickly left as it slows down."

She was right. I could see it now. I stroked the putt and it rolled in like it had eyes. I looked at her and winked. "That was a good read on that putt, thanks."

"I was sure you already saw it. I was just explaining to Ann what you were doing."

Yeah, right.

She smiled and the rest of them finished up.

As we prepared to cart it over to the third hole Ann asked Julie about the GPS system in the carts. "Why is it there? What is it used for?"

"See, there we are and there are the other carts near us. That way we won't hit our ball at anybody. It gives us the distance to the pin, front of the green and back of the green. And here is where we can enter the scores." As Julie explained the features she gave Ann a practical demonstration.

Ann thought a minute and said. "It's really not all that useful, is it? I mean it couldn't even tell us where my first ball went." That was the only thing that mattered to her. "I don't know if I like this, we don't get much exercise sitting in the cart." **[18 holes in a golf cart burns about 1300 calories. Walking 18 will only burn 2000 calories.]**

I enjoyed the remaining sixteen holes and shot a respectable score but not a 72, which was par. None of the others in my group were anywhere close, well that's not totally true. Julie had a pretty good round going until fifteen. She just ran out of gas and had to limit her activity to putting.

It's an old joke but we all got to par, we just got to 72, the magic number, a few holes too soon.

When we were done I wished them all the best and told Julie I'd pray for her. I have no idea how things turned out for her. I never saw them again. They likely went back to Colorado and I continued my pursuit of par or less. I will never forget the 'barely lost' concept though. I also decided to reassess my belief that life is a game and golf is serious. Turns out that may not be accurate.

Listening to Ann ask questions and question things that seemed strange to her, I was reminded of some of the rules of golf we all tend to ignore. If you rub your ball on the green to remove dirt, that is a one stroke penalty. You are not allowed to test the surface of the green. If you are off the green and chipping up but someone is close enough to the flag stick to touch it that is a two stroke penalty. It is deemed that if they can reach the flag stick then they are tending it. And finally, if your playing partner is out of bounds and you hit him or her with an errant shot and the ball ends up out of bounds you may replay the shot with no penalty. These are actual rules.

There are also local rules unique to each course. One course Par-Man frequents has a large screen that protects golfers on a tee box close to the fairway. If you hit behind that screen there is a free drop to the edge of the screen that always gives the golfer a shot at making it to the green in regulation. Hitting a long slice on this hole won't hurt a bit.

At Augusta, home of the Masters, all electronic devices are prohibited. Then there was a course I played in Canada where they requested that you not hit golf balls at the bears. At another course in Canada, near Banff, it is requested that if you plan to drink to excess then please attend a hockey game instead of golfing.

Actual rules and local rules are exactly why some people find this a strange game to play.

Reason two that golf is better than sex:
No one snickers when the postman delivers a golf magazine.

HOLE THREE
The Nemesis

Proper golf etiquette is to let the person with the lowest score tee off first. In case of a tie then go back to the previous hole. Teeing off first is all some people play for. Never hit in front of a birdie, the golf gods don't like that and if your playing partner is hitting from the tips always let them go first. Remember for honors use the score they gave you not what you think they had after the penalty strokes for playing the ball up.

WE ARE NOW GOING TO TRANSPORT OURSELVES to Painted Hills golf course in Kansas City, Kansas. This is a nice course. Not real hard and reasonably fair to the average golfer. What makes this tract remarkable is this was the first time Par-Man achieved his goal of a par round. Oh, I didn't get it but I helped someone else reach golf heaven. I knew I had a shot when the two fellas I was paired with were preparing to tee off from the back tees, or in golf parlance, the tips. They looked like they could be scratch golfers. **[A scratch golfer is one with a zero handicap]**

Now Painted Hills is a very nice, well-kept course. It's just not real long. My playing partners, as I suspected, were good, very good. They were in the middle of the fairway on the first two holes and Hunter, one of the two, birdied the second hole. His friend, Bert, had missed his first two birdie putts and had to settle for tap in pars. With them there were no gimmies. **[Gimmes are essentially an agreement between two golfers, neither of which can putt very well.]**

"You two are really good. Did you play in college?"

Bert, the more talkative one responded. "Yes and we were both on what was once called the Web.com Tour."

I wondered if I should ask the next question and since we were waiting for the group ahead of us to clear the green I decided, why not? "If you don't mind my asking, why are you playing here?"

The implication was that this course was beneath their respective skill levels and would not be much of a challenge for them. Again, it was Bert that answered. "Hunter grew up near here and this was the course where he learned to golf. He hadn't been back in a number of years and wanted to play it one more time."

The bewildered look on my face was clear. That wasn't much of a reason.

"See, Hunter never shot even par or better on this course. The third hole here always did him in and he wants to face his fears." Was this really a case for Par-Man? Time to check further.

Was Bert kidding, I waited for a punch line. Instead, Hunter spoke. "I left Kansas when I was fourteen and we moved to California. This hole," he pointed at the green where the foursome ahead of us was putting out, "has been something I need to face."

These two were as serious as golfers can be. Now I had only seen them play for half an hour but this hole wasn't going to be much of a challenge. It was a par three, medium length at 160 yards, downhill and no sand to deal with. The green was fairly large and reasonably flat.

As I looked over the two men in their early forties were standing stoically by anxious for the green to clear. I thought maybe a golf story might relax them. As I approached I saw their intensity and realized my plan of spreading a little levity was going to blow-up in my face. I couldn't U-turn without looking foolish so I reached down and grabbed some grass to check the wind velocity and direction. The grass I released blew into their faces.

"Sorry." I slinked away. Fortunately the green was clear and it was time to hit.

The two semi-pros were playing the back tees. Because I'm macho and easily embarrassed, I was also playing those tees. I was teeing off last since I had scored the worst on the previous hole. I had a bogey. Bert was first. He had a beautiful, compact swing. His shot sailed straight toward the pin and landed within fifteen feet. Hunter motioned for me to go next.

"Are you sure? You parred the previous hole, you have honors."

"Hunter, hit the damn ball." It was obvious Bert thought this was stupid.

"Okay."

He teed up the ball and stepped back. He addressed the ball and then stepped back again. I found it impossible to believe that someone who had played, even unsuccessfully, in golf's minor leagues could let one, relatively easy hole, intimidate him so.

Hunter walked up and the two of them talked quietly for a moment. Then Hunter looked at me and quietly said, "Go ahead, if you're ready."

"Sure." For me this was a long par three. I needed to use my five iron if I had any hope of hitting the ball the equivalent of a hundred and seventy five yards. Even though it was all downhill there was a one and a half club breeze directly in my face.

It was a beautiful shot, for about the first one hundred yards. Then it started to fade, but it did land on the green nearly twice as far away as Bert's shot was. I was happy though.

"Your turn, Hunter. Just relax and swing away." Bert was trying to be encouraging and supportive but all three of us knew it was patronizing to say the least.

Right here I should interject some information I got later in the round but is germane to this particular hole. It helped me understand why Hunter was having such trouble with the third hole at Painted Hills. But first let me tell you a story.

A priest decided to head out to the golf course at the crack of dawn and skip the early Sunday Mass. The course would be empty and he would be able to get done in time for ten thirty a.m. Mass. God and St. Peter were watching and St. Peter was furious. "He has to be punished for neglecting his flock."

"I agree." Was all God said.

The priest was having the game of his life. He could do no wrong and since he was alone with an empty course ahead of him he was able to develop a smooth and consistent rhythm. He was hitting the ball crisply and cleanly on every swing.

God looked at St. Peter and commented. "He's pretty good, isn't he?"

"That's all you've got to say. He needs to be shown that this is not acceptable behavior."

"I know and I will take care of it."

The round continued and the priest's score got even better. St. Peter was getting angrier and angrier. "I thought you were going to handle this. This is how you handle a priest who skips Mass?"

"Have faith."

"Jesus, that's your answer to everything."

The Lord smiled at the pun. The priest was at the seventeenth hole, a par three, and when he struck the ball it had that sound, the sound that told the priest it was struck well. It hit the green, took two bounces and disappeared into the hole. The priest went crazy and so did St. Peter, both for different reasons.

"You are impossible. I want that priest punished!" St. Peter was yelling at the Creator as the priest finished the round.

"I have."

"How. The man just had a dream round that included a hole-in-one."

"I know." Then God smiled and asked St. Peter. "But who can he tell?"

In a way, that explained Hunter's problem. Out practicing after school he was playing the third hole and aced it. **[The odds of two aces in one round of golf are 1 in 64 million. John Hudson did just that in 1971 at a tournament in Norwich, England.]** He was thrilled. He went home but no one ever quite believed him. His coach told him that unless he played all eighteen holes it wasn't a recordable ace. The members of his golf team scoffed and when his mom got involved, his dad had been killed in Iraq, things became even worse.

It sounds all philosophical and weird but golf is a game played in the head as well as on the course. The head part was giving Hunter problems.

"There were several more high school matches played at this course but every time Hunter came to the third hole he tried so hard to do well that he did awful." Bert explained this to me several holes later.

Back to the third hole tee box. Hunter teed up and had an iron in his hands.

"Just relax." Bert was trying to be supportive. **[Ben Hogan was known to be a bit cantankerous and when someone suggested he should relax he responded, 'Relax, I have to grip the club don't I?']**

You could see it was going to be a disaster. Bert was rigid as a board. The muscles in his arms were tight and he was practically choking the club. Now, if you think I stepped in here and said or did something to solve Hunter's problem, well, you're wrong. Do not give unsolicited advice is one of golf's unwritten rules.

No, the golf gods stepped in and solved the problem. Many golf courses have a common problem. They try to solve this common problem with fake owls, cutouts of foxes and even live dogs. The problem: geese that don't ever fly south. They live on the course, lay eggs, raise their young, crap all over the course, chew-up the greens and even attack golfers.

One of these annoying critters started walking across the green just as Hunter took his last look at his target and he backed away.

Bert jumped on the opportunity. "You know that they can't do anything to the geese physically to move them off the greens but we can take them out. Go ahead. See if you can hit it."

I know that sounds cruel but if you've ever seen what geese do to a green you'd understand. Hunter had seen it, Bert had seen it and I had seen it. Bert looked at me so I helped egg him on. "Go ahead Hunter. If you actually hit the damn thing it will start squawking and draw all the other geese to his aid. They will then honk encouragement to their wounded comrade."

I had actually witnessed that very thing when a playing partner of mine nailed a goose with a low line drive. He didn't do it on purpose. It was a mishit. Within a minute there were dozens of geese around the injured one honking encouragement to the fallen goose. It worked. The nasty fowl eventually popped back up and flew away.

Bert had screwed up his mouth and gave me a look that said, *"That's not helpful."*

He was right. We didn't need or want any more of those filthy birds on the green.

Hunter laughed at my dumb comment. Stepped up and hit his seven iron onto the green about eight feet from the pin. The mental block had been lifted. All three of us parred the hole. Bert and Hunter ended their rounds at one under and two under respectively. Par-Man had achieved his goal. Play with someone and help them get to even par or better. Unfortunately Par-Man ended up in the 80's. Oh, well there was always next weekend.

One other interesting little tidbit, both of them had played with Ryan Armour, son of Tommy Armour, and said that he was part of the reason they gave up on golf as a career. His focus, drive and practice schedule were way more than they were prepared for and he wasn't even a big money winner. Their skill levels were a little different but Ryan's intensity was way different. According to Hunter and Bert the difference is the level of commitment each golfer is willing to make, every single day.

Did you know it's a rule that if a golfer hits a shot that ricochets off a tree or any other object and hits him then he is assessed a two stroke penalty. If he hits another golfer he isn't assessed any penalty but may face other problems, especially if the other golfer is a lawyer.

You heard about the golfer who had an early tee time every Saturday. He was a fanatic and sometimes played 36 holes. This one Saturday, at 6 a.m., he eased out of bed so as not to wake his wife, went to the garage, put his golf clubs and shoes in the car and looked outside. It was pouring rain, windy and worse, the weather was going to continue like this for several hours. Waiting to see if the storm passed the disappointed man, after an hour, eventually gave up. He took his golf apparel off and crawled back into bed, put his arms around his wife and said, "The weather is terrible. I'm here for you."

She replied, "That's fine but can you believe my idiot husband is out golfing in this shit?"

Reason three that golf is better than sex:
Your wife won't care if pictures of you golfing show up on Facebook.

HOLE FOUR
THE TEACHER

Proper golf etiquette and safety concerns make it imperative that after an errant shot the golfer warns others by yelling 'fore.' Others in the group may have to do the honors if the ball striker gets lockjaw after his horrid miscue. If you do hit into a group immediately apologize and let them know you yelled fore. It will help you in court if there are any serious damages.

FALCON LAKES IS NORTHWEST OF KANSAS CITY. It is one of my twenty favorite courses. For Par-Man it is challenging without being so hard he can't enjoy the round. Playing there is made more enjoyable thanks to the people who work there. If I call up to get a tee time they remember my name and try to pair me with other golfers of a similar skill level.

How do they do that you ask? Well, they know their customers. It was late fall and a little nippy but not too bad. I called in and Gene said, "The wind isn't very strong but it's out of the north. You know what that means."

I did. "Thanks Gene. Have you got a time for me in an hour?"

"I'll work something out."

That meant I should come to the course and he would help me get my round in. The wind out of the north meant that the course would play very different form the summer, when the wind is out of the south and west. **[A tee shot will travel eight yards further for every increase of 25 degrees.]**

True to his word I got off with a twosome as soon as I got there. The two men were named Henry and Wilson. Henry became

Hammerin' Hank after Hank Aaron, Henry was black and Wilson, a white guy, wore glasses that reminded me of Woodrow Wilson. Hell, there were only two names. Surely, I could remember two names.

I might as well tell you that after three holes I knew that Henry and Wilson were not going to shoot par or better. That's not exactly true. They both would get to par, probably about hole fifteen. But as is almost always the case they were really nice guys.

When we approached the fourth hole I was actually looking forward to it. Par-Man was only one over by the time we got to four. Normally the wind would be blowing right in my face and this, almost four hundred yard hole, would be almost impossible for me to par. Today the wind was with me. It was at my back.

"You have honors." It was Henry. He wasn't with the rules police but he did care about who had the box and understood the importance of good golf manners.

"Thank you." I teed up. Tried to relax and hit something with some altitude on it so the wind could carry it. I achieved my goal. It was a magnificent shot, in the middle and only a buck twenty five from the pin. I was ecstatic.

Their shots, not so great. As I waited for them to get within range of the green I thought of an incident that had occurred while golfing with my dad and brother.

We were on a par five at the green. It was a 'Z' shaped par five that required three perfect shots to get to the green. If you were a big hitter you might be able to cut the corners and save a stroke or even two.

The three of us were standing on the green waiting for dad, who was away, to putt first. Just after he struck his putt a ball came screaming in from behind us. "Dad, look out!"

It missed him by several yards but really angered my brother. "Who the hell hit that? No one yelled fore." Looking at me he asked. "Did you hear anyone yell?"**[Fore is believed to be an abbreviation of the Scottish 'afore' meaning ahead. There are also those who think it comes from when there were fore-caddies. Because golf balls in the eighteenth century were hard to make and very expensive, they placed caddies ahead of the golfer so if his shot**

was errant, they could spot it and find the ball. Fore was yelled to let the caddies ahead know the ball was coming.]

"No, I didn't." I was aggravated too. I was hit by a golf ball once and it hurt like hell. It wasn't intentional but it didn't lessen the pain. But none of us were hit and for that I was thankful. Since no one was laying on the green, unconscious, I was willing to wait and see who came forward.

Dad was the only one who actually watched where the mistimed shot went. It hit the green and rolled toward the pin. Dad's silence caught our attention. We looked. The ball came to rest a foot from the hole. Dad walked over and kicked it in. My brother and I were shocked. It wasn't like dad to do something like that.

"A guy that can hit a shot like that deserves to be rewarded." Dad shrugged as he made the comment.

Before we could say anything else a cart came barreling up toward us with two people in it, a man and a woman. "I am so sorry. So sorry. Is everyone all right?"

"You could have killed him." It was my brother talking to the guy driving the cart who had offered the apology.

"I had no idea it would go that far. I just hit where they told me. I've never played here before." It was the woman talking now. The three of us were stunned.

Dad walked over and looked at her and said, "We are all fine. It was a great shot. Don't apologize for a great shot."

She smiled and said, "Thanks. Where is my ball?"

"That's the thing young lady. It rolled into the hole. It was a great shot. It came over the trees, hit the green and rolled right in. What does that give you? Birdie, eagle, what?"

She looked confused. The man next to her spoke. "An eight."

Henry and Wilson were now within range and it was my turn. My second shot was just as good as my first. I was now about six feet from a birdie.

"Wow, great shot." Henry wasn't just being polite. He was genuinely impressed, as was Wilson. When we got to the green they asked me if I wanted to putt first so I didn't have to wait.

"No, that's all right. You're away, go ahead and putt." Often when I played I was the least skilled of the group. Today I was most skilled, and by a fair amount. I was rather enjoying it.

The two of them putted until they had enough. Neither of them had any touch on the green. Slope, break and distance, none of it came into play when they would putt. They got within a few feet and picked up.

Now it was my turn. Henry and Wilson waited. They were as anxious as I was. Dead center. I had my birdie. The two of them were almost as ecstatic as me, almost.

So far this doesn't seem like a terribly funny or poignant hole. It was what happened after the birdie that stuck with me.

Henry came over, before we left the green, and asked. "Could you show me how you putt?"

I looked at him quizzically.

"You've seen me putt and I'm awful. I know I'll never be a good golfer but I'd like to play without embarrassing myself."

"Henry, I'm not really that great a putter."

"You're way better than I am." His facial expression was clear, *please help me.*

As I said earlier it was a bit nippy **[Woodrow Wilson played golf in the snow using a black golf ball, he really loved the game.]** and the course was not busy. We stood on the fourth hole for fifteen minutes and practiced. He and Wilson both improved in just fifteen minutes.

For the next fourteen holes the two of them discussed every putt. Henry would say, "No E. J. said to putt through the ball, don't hit at it."

I, Par-Man, was being quoted. I knew that they were never going have a par round and today, unfortunately, neither was I. The PBFU took over and I double bogeyed the next hole. (Post Birdie Foul Up)

When the round was over the two men thanked me profusely and congratulated me on being such and accomplished golfer. Me. Accomplished. Who would have guessed it?

Speaking of putting I will tell you how I got tricked on the green. A 'friend' I was playing with put a ball six inches from the hole. He then put a second ball two inches behind the first one. He said. "I'll bet you I can putt the second ball into the cup and never touch the first one."

I studied the situation and couldn't see how he could make this claim. He couldn't go around. The green was pretty flat. There was no way to put any spin on it. Ah-ha, I knew what he was going to do.

"You're going to use the end of the putter like a pool cue and hit the lower half of the ball and get it to jump over the first ball."

"Nope. I'll use a normal putting stroke."

"Okay, I'll take the bet." What we bet is unimportant, because it's embarrassing.

He lined up behind the second ball, putted like the first ball wasn't even there and stroked his putt. The second ball hopped right over the first ball and rolled into the cup.

"How did you do that?"

Once we settled our wager he showed me. After he originally placed the two balls on the green and while I was walking around trying to figure out the trick he used his foot and pushed down on the second ball. It was now resting in a small crater. When he stroked the putt he angled the putter head back so it had some loft. By hitting the second ball crisply it jumped over the first ball and into the cup.

If someone tries to trick you like that you'll be prepared.

Some other words of wisdom related to putting. 1) When the greens are really fast all you need to do is hold your putter over the ball and hit it with the shadow. 2) The problem with most of us is after we putt we are still standing too close to the ball. 3) Just like sex you can't be concentrating on the mechanics while you are trying to perform.

*Reason four that golf is better than sex:
A golf lesson isn't going to turn into an undercover sting.*

HOLE FIVE
Doctor, Please

Proper golf etiquette and common sense should dictate how you dress. Country clubs will likely be more demanding than the local municipal course, call ahead when in doubt. In any case sleeveless tee shirts that say 'bitchin' on the front are never appropriate. Plaids, stripes and garish colors are all acceptable if done in good taste. That may be an oxymoron.

TIFFANY GREENS IS A FIRST-CLASS COURSE in Missouri near the Kansas City Airport. Over the years it has hosted several tour events for the seniors and is a reasonably difficult par 72. **[The longest golf course in the world is 8,325 yards and is located in Massachusetts, the International Golf Club.]**Par-Man had decided to give it a try and took a day off work to play. It was the only time they would accept a single.

I got a beautiful day and Par-Man was looking forward to a new course. Before arriving he used Google Earth to look at the course and get a feel for how difficult it would be. It was more difficult than expected. By the fifth hole all hope of the perfect round had been dashed. There were already two lost balls that led to two double bogeys.

"This is a lot tougher than I had expected when I looked at the score card on line and pulled up the course on Google Earth." I was talking to Ronald. That was how he introduced himself so I assumed he didn't want me calling him Ron or Ronnie or any other derivative of Ronald. He had on very red shorts and a yellow shirt so, you guessed it, he was Ronald McDonald. I had no trouble remembering his name.

His friend, Don, responded to my statement. "It's the elevation changes." My dad's name was Don so that one was easy as well.

"Yeah, they're something." I agreed. The fifth hole was only 348 yards but it must rise sixty feet from tee box to green. There is a sand trap on the left at about two twenty and several more up by the green.

"You better be pretty good to par this hole." That was Lucas. A tall man, that I immediately equated to The Rifleman, Lucas McCain. A western series on in the sixties, it was in black and white. **[Lucas McCain's real name was Chuck Connors and he was a professional basketball player before he got into acting.]**

We all agreed this was a tough one. To put it in perspective this was the number 15 handicap hole. We were in for a long day.

My three playing partners were all doctors. Their fourth had an emergency surgery so I was able to join them. They were nice enough, a little quiet, all in their early forties and had the most expensive equipment I had ever seen. I found out that each of their sets were custom made.

The four of them, which included the one in surgery, had gone to the Calloway factory to get fitted and play some golf. It was an expensive trip. According to Ronald they all spent in excess of six grand for their clubs. I guess they have all their student loans already paid off.

It was a Wednesday afternoon and warm, over eighty, and windy. On this hole the wind was right at us. Discussing our common plight we agreed that it would take a two hundred and fifty yard drive to get to the first trap. I could hit anything I wanted.

"That landing area left of the forward trap will give you the best approach to the green." Ronald knew what he was going to do. **[The eighth hole at Whistling Straits in Wisconsin has 102 bunkers.]**

"You're an idiot. First you can't hit it that far and second you will have to clear the trap right in front of the green to get to the pin." Lucas was not hesitant about expressing his opinion.

By the way did I mention that they had started with the beer as soon as we teed off? No one was drunk but I think they had consumed enough alcohol to erase their inhibitions. It was only ten in the morning.

"You two have no idea what you're talking about. Let's see what E. J. thinks." They all turned and looked in my direction.

Now I'm not shy and have no problem expressing my opinion but I didn't want to listen to bickering for thirteen more holes.

"Here's what I think." I teed up the ball and swung. I really didn't care where it went but after it landed all I had to do was come up with a reason why I hit it there. The golf gods smiled and I went right down the middle. Sometimes you just get lucky.

"I like to follow Tiger Woods advice, 'when in doubt go for the middle.'" I have no idea if Tiger ever said that and if he did was he even talking about golf, but I was betting they didn't either.

Don, Ronald and then Lucas teed off. They all did the same thing I did, went for the middle. Two were slightly longer than I was and one quite a bit shorter. The trouble started on the next shot, for all of us. There were six traps on hole five and we found four of them. These were deep traps with lots of nice fluffy sand. It reminded me of a story I once heard.

An older man, late sixties, wanted to join a fairly exclusive country club and to do so he had to play eighteen holes with the club pro.

"Now just relax. We want to be sure that you understand the rules of golf etiquette and won't hold up the other members." The pro, Herbert, wanted Lionel to be comfortable.

"I understand. I should tell you I have a lot of trouble getting out of sand traps."

"Many people do."

The pro parred the first two holes and Lionel parred one of them. On the third hole Lionel hit a terrific tee shot but at the last second it rolled into a sand trap. The old man dug in, swung and hit the ball within a few feet of the cup.

"I thought you said you had trouble getting out of traps?"

"I do. Now help me out."

The next five minutes were just plain butt-ugly. I took two shots to get to the green, one out of the trap and then a chip on to the green. I then waited for what seemed like an eternity for the other three.

Ronald was swearing up a storm. I was in the military and Ronald could hold his own with any of the drill instructors I ran into. On the green, at long last, Lucas said, "Jeez Ronald, a real golfer wouldn't swear like that."

"Of course not! A real golfer would have been on in two and have nothing to swear about. Lucas you can be a real putz." Ronald was exceedingly mad.

Don tried to make peace. "Well we're all on now." Talk about a hollow statement. Ronald looked like he wanted to beat Don to death with his putter.

Time for Par-Man to come to the rescue. "You know a well-made sand trap is actually quite a work of art. They dig much deeper than you think and put in several drains depending on the size of the trap. They then put in some large gravel followed by some pea size gravel. The next step is really interesting. They coat the pea gravel with an epoxy type solution that dries hard and essentially fuses all the gravel together. It can't settle. That promotes proper drainage for years."

Two blank stares and one "Uh-huh."

It did bring the heated discussion to an end. I couldn't leave well enough alone though. "Did you know that Whistling Straits in Wisconsin has 967 sand traps?" **[Pine Valley Course in New Jersey boasts the world's biggest bunker known as 'Hell's Half Acre.']**

Lucas looked at Ronald and said. "See, it could be way worse."

I expected Ronald to explode. Instead he just shook his head and walked over to his ball and prepared to putt. "Yeah, it could have been worse. I could have sliced it into the woods over there."

That reminded me of a story about a slice. I decided to tell it. "There was a lady out golfing and on a hole with houses nearby she sliced her tee shot through the owner's picture window. She was mortified and went over to apologize. To her surprise the owner was sitting on his couch looking relaxed. There was glass everywhere and a broken bottle on the floor."

"She started with a heartfelt apology but before she got very far he held up his hand. He told her not to worry. He was actually a genie and had been in the bottle, now broken and on the floor, for years. Her golf ball freed him. She had three wishes coming."

"Startled, she first asked for a house in Rome. He snapped his fingers and told her it was done. She then asked for enough money so she could travel and never have to work. Again with a snap of his fingers he assured her it was done. But before she used her third wish he had a request."

"I've been in that bottle for a very long time and haven't had the pleasure of a woman's company. Would you do me the honor?"

"After thinking about it she agreed and they went upstairs. They enjoyed each other for several hours. When he was done he asked her how old she was."

"A little surprised and embarrassed at his forwardness she hesitated and the finally answered. 'I'm 35. Why?'"

"His reply, 'That's pretty old to still believe in genies.'"

Don started laughing. I don't think Lucas got it. No matter the tension between them was gone. Par-Man to the rescue.

No one was anywhere near par that day. I did get some free medical advice when I asked Ronald's opinion on a problem I was having. "Sometimes after eighteen holes my back gets stiff and I need a couple of aspirin to relieve the pain. Do you have any suggestions?"

"How old are you?"

"66"

"Lose some weight; get more exercise and if the aspirin work just keep taking them. Anything else?"

"Nope, thanks."

Later I found out that Ronald was an urologist. Oh well, when you ask for free advice you usually get what you pay for.

Reason five that golf is better than sex:
Being part of a foursome is perfectly acceptable.

HOLE SIX
ADAM

Proper golf etiquette on the green is too stay out of the line of sight of the person who is putting. Watch your shadow and stand still. The rules forbid standing directly in line with a putt to gage its break. And never wave the flagstick like you are surrendering even if you feel like giving up.

THIS HOLE WAS THE CULMINATION of one of my strangest encounters. A course, Sunflower Hills in Kansas, I frequent has what are called starter times. They use those times to put walk-ons and singles like me together. If no one fills those spots then play moves along a little more quickly.

"E. J. you are going off at 8:51. You will be with three other guys." The god controlling the course, the starter, had spoken.

We all met at the number one tee box a few minutes before the appointed time. I actually can't remember the names of two of the golfers but I do recall the fourth player, Adam. I'll refer to the other members of our foursome as One and Two. This was a number years ago before I invented my name memory system.

One, was very quiet and spoke very softly. Two, was somewhat gregarious and always seemed to be in motion. Adam was aloof. He only nodded when we all introduced ourselves. He looked like he took the game fairly seriously. When the number one fairway was clear Adam walked right up to the box and prepared to tee-off. He had a nice practice swing and clearly had played the game before.

The ball rocketed off the face of his club. It went a nifty two hundred plus and just crept into the rough, which wasn't all that long. It looked like they had mowed yesterday. We complemented him on his shot, to be polite, and because it was a good drive.

"I should have been in the fairway and twenty yards further. What the hell am I doing? That shot sucks." Adam wasn't talking to us but seemed to be talking to an imaginary friend. He was unhappy with a shot that any of us would have taken in a heartbeat. Oh, well.

I should mention that we were all walking. It was in the high sixties and slightly overcast. After the rest of us teed off Two scurried over to One and they started walking together. I looked around to walk with Adam. He was already twenty yards down the fairway marching toward his ball. It was a strident march that I had no intention of matching. I went toward my ball at my pace.

Golf etiquette says that you all stop at the shortest ball and let that person hit. First, it keeps everyone out of harm's way since they are behind the person hitting. Second, they are out of the golfers' line of sight and that prevents any distractions. Adam, who was long, marched on until he got to his ball. Maybe he wasn't afraid of getting boinked by a golf ball.

As Par-Man, I didn't want anybody to get hurt so I yelled, "Adam, heads up." And I pointed to One who had ended up short. Adam ignored my warning. Two spoke up. "Maybe he didn't hear you."

He heard me and he chose to ignore me. If it affected One he didn't show it. He hit his second shot without regard to where Adam was. The shot was straight and no one got boinked. We all hit, even though Adam was ahead of us. Eventually we caught up to Adam and stopped to let him hit.

"Now hit this like you should. Don't let all these distractions upset you." He was talking to his imaginary partner but I think we were the distractions he was referring to.

Adam had about a buck and half to the green. He hit a beautiful shot that was just a bit past pin high. As we all made our way to the green Adam was still talking. "You dummy. Why did you hit that long? Just relax don't let the others distract you." He wasn't yelling but he wasn't whispering either. We all could hear him but he wasn't actually talking to any of us.

Adam easily parred the hole. The rest of us bogeyed the hole. There was still hope for someone to achieve the perfect round. Strangely I found myself almost rooting against Adam.

The second hole was similar. Adam bitched about everything he did and inferred we were somehow the reason he wasn't performing like he thought he should. It was a par five and again Adam parred the hole as did Par-Man. One and Two had bogeys.

The third hole was a par four and after his drive Adam was only an eight iron away. **[The eight iron was originally called the pitching niblick.]** Adam was the last to hit his second shot because he had the longest drive. His ball came to rest twenty or so feet from the flagstick. Two was very complementary. "Wow, nice shot. That was such a smooth swing. I wish I could hit the ball like that."

Adam looked at him and replied. "It's left too far and there was no backspin. That's a nearly impossible birdie putt. Why would you want to hit the ball like that?"

The fourth hole was uneventful mostly because it was a par three and Adam hit a very good tee shot and birdied the hole. There wasn't anything for Adam to complain about.

This went on at every hole to varying degrees. Sometimes Adam was completely silent and other times he chewed himself out and indirectly blamed us for his perceived lack of performance. He golfed well and was somewhere near par as we approached the sixth hole.

To give you a point of reference the sixth hole at Sunflower is the number one handicap hole. For anyone that doesn't know that means it is the hardest hole on the course. It's a par five around five hundred and fifty yards. **[The current method of handicapping holes using slope and a course rating didn't really get any traction until the mid-1960's]**

On number six we all got off the tee pretty well but Adam got off exceptionally well. After we all hit our second shots Adam prepared to hit his second as well. He pulled out a three wood and looked like he was going to try and crush one up to the green.

I have no idea what he did but Adam's shot sliced something awful, it was way left and disappeared into the trees. The club went into the air and the verbal barrage began. "Why didn't you check that ball? You know what happens. All you had to do was look. You are such a dumb shit."

I was willing to let it go but Two had to ask. "What did you forget to check?"

Adam stared at Two like he was an idiot. In a tone meant to convey his frustration with having to explain something so obvious he spoke. "Sometimes, when you swing like I do, the ball gets out of round. I think that's what happened." **[Tiger Woods has a swing speed over 130 mph and he can't hit a ball out of round.]**

Two looked at me and I just shrugged. One ignored the entire conversation. On the green One actually parred the hole by sinking a rather long putt. Adam offered no congratulatory words.

As Adam prepared to putt he continued to speak to his invisible partner. "Don't let all of this ruin your round. Ignore them."

One dropped his putter right there on the green and turned toward Adam. I don't think Adam even knew that One was preparing to confront him. One was nearly on top of Adam before he saw what was happening. His instinct was to retreat but One just kept coming. Inches from Adam's face One spoke. I think it was the first words he had said since the round began.

"If you say another damn word I swear to God I will kill you and throw your dead body in the woods where you and your out of round golf ball can rot for all eternity."

He turned and marched toward the seventh tee.

Adam was actually appalled but he obviously didn't take the threat seriously because he started talking before One was three steps away. "I wasn't talking to you. I just talk to myself sometimes. I don't mean anything by it. I just have high expectations for myself."

It was time for Par-Man to step in. "I think this would be a good time to be quiet." What I really wanted to say would serve no useful purpose so I kept my thoughts in my head. Something I hoped Adam would do for the next twelve holes.

It didn't happen. Adam never let up, but we all just ignored him and talked amongst ourselves. One actually became more interactive after he said his piece to Adam. When the eighteenth hole was in the books we all shook hands, including Adam. Then the weirdest thing happened and considering how the day went, that's saying a lot.

"Hey, I really enjoyed playing with you guys. I don't have a regular group to play with. If I give you my number would you give me a call the next time you want to play?" Adam's tone was begging for someone to take him up on his offer. I couldn't let the poor bastard stand there like that.

Par-Man to the rescue. "Sure, give me your number."

One and Two looked at me like I'd spent too much time in the sun. Because of my secret identity they didn't know I was a super-hero. Adam smiled broadly and wrote his number on my scorecard. I lost the damn thing though and never called. Oh, well.

There are many unwritten golf rules. One is golfers should be seen and not heard. **[While sad, the golf gods have a way of dealing with a rip in the Force, the golf Force that is, as shown by what happened to a man who, in a fit of anger, died when he broke his club on a bench and the shaft pierced his heart. This took place at the Kingsboro Golf Club, on the sixth hole. Coincidence?]**

A small point but while I have never heard of a golf ball being out of round I did see one where the cover cracked, just slightly. The ball had been in the trunk of this particular golfer's car all winter. The day we played it was just above freezing. He swears that it sounded funny when he struck it. A close inspection revealed a hairline fracture of the cover. But out of round, I don't think so.

Reason six that golf is better than sex:
Golf has no STDs.

HOLE SEVEN
The Champion

Proper golf etiquette is not to assume anything: Ask. Do you want the flag in, can you see the cup, is my mark in the way, do I talk too much? Ask, it will stave-off all sorts of problems.

TOMAHAWK GOLF COURSE is within walking distance of Par-Man's house. One Sunday evening I walked down there and was going to play nine before dark. The course was empty and given some luck I might actually get a few extra holes in.

I got through the first six in forty-five minutes. As I approached seven there was another golfer on the tee box. As I got closer I saw it was a woman.

Now I will be the first to admit that my initial reaction to seeing her was that this was probably a lousy golfer out on her own so she doesn't get embarrassed in a group. I'm not proud of the fact that those were my first thoughts but it was the truth. As a courtesy I asked if she wanted to join up. I fully expected her to tell me to play through.

"I'd like that. Some competition might help me play with some intensity." An answer I wasn't prepared for.

"Okay." I walked up to the white tees and hit a fairly nice shot about two twenty just left of center.

She walked back to the tips, the blue tees, and prepared to tee off. "I'm sorry. I just thought, you know, that you were playing the reds." One of golf's unwritten rules is to let the person playing the deepest set of tees go first. It's a convenience thing.

"It's all right, it happens all the time." She smiled and proceeded to hit a tee shot thirty yards past mine.

"Wow, nice shot." I was impressed.

"Do you still want to team up?" Her look told me she was aware that the male ego was as fragile as a Ming Dynasty vase.

"You bet. But I have some questions, if that's all right?"

"Sure."

Now, if you think this hole is about some terrific golfer who happens to be a woman, you would only be partially right. If you think this hole is about some male golfer with preconceived ideas about women golfers being taught a lesson in humility then, again, you would be partially right. The real story of this hole is why the two reasons just mentioned come to mind first.

Men tend to have the preconceived idea that women can't be good golfers. Even women have that idea. Par-Man taught his daughter to golf and she had one request. "Dad, don't let me hit the ball like a girl."

Four women finished their round. Sitting at the nineteenth hole, they were bragging. The first woman smiled and said, "I had fifteen riders."

Number two said, "I had twenty-one."

The third lady was proud of her twenty-six riders but number four was saddened by her sixteen riders.

When they left I asked the bartender what a rider was. He laughed.

"A rider is when they hit the ball far enough that they can get in the cart and ride to the ball."

This is typical of how men tend to see women golfers. When we come across one that is good we are surprised, then intimidated. **[In 1962, Sam Snead became the only male golfer to win an LPGA tournament. He won the Poinciana Plaza Invitational by five strokes. Babe Zaharias is the only woman to ever make the cut at a PGA Tour event. It happened at the L.A. Open in 1945.]**

It might be this way because of history. Going back to the Old Course at St. Andrew's the caddies were given a putting green next to the 17th hole. When women started showing an interest in the sport they actually displaced the caddies and took the putting green as their own. When the men first began allowing women to play they would only allow them to carry one club, a putter.

The involvement of women in golf may go back further than people think. Though there are references to women playing golf in 15th century, and other related stick and ball games, care needs to be taken as these may not refer to golf or to the game as we know it.

The first credible mention of women playing golf is at Bruntsfield Links in 1738 and the first reference to links golf is in 1811 at Musselburgh, though women's golf societies were not formed until the last quarter of the 19th century. Then came an explosion of interest in women's golf and golf clubs. **[Links courses are characterized by thin strips of grass, sand and dunes. These courses usually have few trees, undulating fairways and lots of bunkers.]**

Significant events for golf history include the formation of LGU, Ladies Golf Union, in 1893, the first UK golfing association, and the creation of a proper national handicapping system, which the men's associations would, by and large, subsequently adopt.

Mary, Queen of Scots was the first to suggest the use of caddies in the 16th century. She had a military cadet, the first caddy, carry her clubs. When Mary studied in France she brought her enthusiasm for the game with her. They loved it instantly.

Now, we go back to the woman in the fairway on the seventh hole. Her approach was a beautiful arching shot that landed softly ten feet from the cup. Par-Man missed the green but chipped on and ended up six feet away.

"Nice chip."

"Yeah, but I should have been on in two. I just yanked it."

"A Mickey Mantle, huh?" She knew the lingo. Billy Martin, Yogi Berra and Roger Maris are all dead Yanks, hence the reference.

She parred the hole only because she lipped out on her birdie putt. I parred the hole but only because I got a good read on her putt.

"Nice par." She seemed generally happy that I parred the hole.

"Not like yours. On in two and a tap in for par, it's the way they draw them up."

"A four is a four. There aren't any pictures or style points. At the end of the day it's all about the score, nothing else." It appeared, based on her tone that was a lesson she was still learning.

I will not use this woman's real name but if you look at the plaque on the wall of the clubhouse you will see one woman has won the championship several times. That's her. As the round continued she told me the story of how she became such a terrific golfer.

She had married fairly late in life and she and her husband had no children. About two years ago he took a job where he traveled quite a bit and she was restless. He suggested golf and she took one lesson and fell in love. For a year she took a lesson every other day.

"Really?"

She smiled. "I know that seems extreme but I played tennis and softball when I was in college and everything about golf came fairly easy to me."

Having watched her play half a round of golf it was obvious. **[She used forged head which use softer steel and provide a better feel as long as you hit the sweet spot. The pros all use forged heads. Oh yeah, the sweet spot on a forged head is a circle about a quarter of an inch in diameter.]**

"I'm headed to Phoenix tomorrow to play in a Pro-Am. I wanted to get some practice in."

"Am I screwing you up?"

"Heavens, no. There will be some really awful players there. I will need to be able to keep my concentration." After she made that statement my reaction must have conveyed what I was thinking. Par-Man was how she practiced for playing with really awful golfers.

"I didn't mean you. I'm so sorry if you thought that I was..."

I was laughing. I didn't care if she meant me or not. She was an excellent golfer and I was not. Facts are facts. "It's fine. I'm not taking it personal. Besides, I was the one who asked the question.

[Like 90% of golfers I use cast clubs with cavity backs. The sweet spot on this type of club is an inch in diameter.]

Even though we only got nine holes in it was a very pleasurable half-round. She was extremely pleasant and even gave me some pointers. Because she was so observant my weak grip was strengthened and my shots after that were much straighter.

The nine ended with my partner at two under and Par-Man was four over. But hey, this was counted as another success for Par-Man. Being a super-hero has its moments.

Reason seven that golf is better than sex:
It's all right to find a new partner if your current one loses interest.

HOLE EIGHT
Oh, God

Proper golf etiquette requires that you consider your audience before telling, religious, ethnic, gender oriented or political jokes. In other words no jokes until you know if you'll be apologizing when you're finished. Trust me, the rest of the round will seem really long if you don't know your audience.

DID YOU HEAR THE ONE about the golfer whose tee shot went awry and hit a priest. The man ran over and started apologizing profusely.

"I'm fine, don't worry." Said the cleric.

The man looked at the priest and asked, "Are you sure?"

"Yes, I'm fine, like I told you. You can now tell your friends that you finally got a holy one."

For some inexplicable reason, the clergy and golf have made a good team when it comes to jokes. Bars and politics are the only things that have been better fodder for stand-up comics and jokesters.

A priest who loved golf flew to Scotland to play St. Andrews. It had been a dream of his and to get the full experience a caddy was hired to help with course management. Not doing too well the priest was incredibly frustrated. On the seventh hole his tee shot found the lake. He had reached his breaking point.

"I'm going to walk over to that lake and drown myself."

The caddy responded. "I don't think you can do that."

"Why?"

"I don't believe you can keep your head down long enough."

In many ways this eighth hole at St. Andrews in Overland Park, Kansas was the embodiment of golf/clergy humor. It has nothing to do with the fact that eight is a fairly easy par four. **[The number one oxymoron in golf-it's an easy par three.]** There is one sand trap about half way to the green, some woods on left and a green that's three times as wide as it is deep. The physical aspects of the hole mean nothing. This is about Par-Man's playing partners.

We all introduced ourselves on the first hole. The short, somewhat portly gentleman, named Norman became the Norman on Cheers. I would remember his cart mates name easily. The passenger in the cart is the sidekick and the Lone Ranger's side kick was Tonto. Tonto's real name was Jay Silverheel and Norm's side kick was named Jay. See how easy this system is? Finally, there was Stan and since he was a walker and always stan-ding, well you get the picture.

When we got to the eighth hole the group ahead of us was waiting for the group on the green. Things had come to a screeching halt. As is often the case when there is down time the group will ask each other questions. You know, 'how long have you been golfing,' 'ever had a hole-in-one,' 'what do you do when you're not practicing for the Tour'?

To get the ball rolling Par-Man asked a general question. "Do you all live near here?"

The three men looked at each other then at me. I didn't think they were going to answer the question. Were they hit men? Norman spoke. "Now don't get all weird on us but I'm a priest and Jay is a Lutheran minister and Stan…"

"If you tell me Stan is a rabbi I'm leaving." I wouldn't really but it was a dramatic thing to say.

Norman laughed. "No, Stan is my brother. My biological brother not a religious brother." Now it was my turn to laugh.

Up until this revelation I had been myself, meaning some words slipped out that probably wouldn't have passed my lips had I known from the beginning that I was with a priest and a minister. Oh yeah, and a brother. I asked why they didn't say something earlier so I could have avoided embarrassing myself.

"We used to, but the other players became so self-conscious that it was stressful for all of us. Sometimes we lie and tell another player, if they even ask, that we are in education." Jay was talking while Norman wrestled with something in his bag.

I could see where their callings might increase the anxiety in a game already fraught with tension. "I get that but if I were prone to swearing, you know like lots of swearing, and then I found out later you were in the religious profession it could be really awkward."

Norman was done fooling around with his bag after retrieving some water (was it holy water) and spoke. "It does come up when we make a small cross with the tees and pray at the turn."

Stan chimed in. "It's not a small cross." He then looked at me and continued. "It's fairly large and they put it on the tenth tee by sticking thirty or so tees in the ground. He prays," looking at Jay, "and he blesses them." Now he's looking at his brother, Norm, the priest.

I had no idea what to say. Before I spit out something completely stupid the group in the fairway made their way to the green and we could tee off. As I drove down the fairway I wondered how priests and ministers relieve the tension of a bad shot. Most golfers groan or curse or throw a club. It would be unseemly for men of God to do that.

I got my answer when Jay's second shot hit the only branch anywhere near his ball and it ended up only ten yards closer to the green. **[We can hit a three acre fairway 20% of the time and a two inch branch 80% of the time.]** He turned and looked skyward, closed his eyes and held that pose for thirty seconds or so. I asked what he was doing.

"I told the Lord that his will, not mine, shall prevail but if wasn't a big deal to Him could He, just once, let me have things my way." Then he smiled wryly and continued. "Actually I told him I was majorly pissed and if he didn't help me then I was going to make a deal with the devil."

They were a fun threesome and we had an enjoyable time even though none of us shot par or better. Well, maybe next time. There was no cross or praying at the tenth hole, for which I was relieved and when Norman finished his bottle of water I was pretty sure it was just ordinary water.

The priest and minister did tell me they had one advantage over me by being in the clergy, the quality of their equipment. The priest, Norm, had especially nice gear. "The parishioners are always wondering what to get us for birthdays and such so I tell them take up a collection and I'll get some fitted clubs. From that point on I get either gift cards to Dick's or Golf Galaxy every year."

Stan chimed in. "Last year he went to Firestone Country Club in Akron and played. He did pretty well. The man that took him wanted to get the same clubs, balls, tees, everything. Norm looked at him and said, 'it won't be the same without the faith.' Nodding solemnly the man walked away."

"I died laughing. I never got to use the punch line. He was supposed to ask me if that really helps. I would say 'not nearly as much as lessons and some skill' but he just turned and left." Norm was remembering the incident and clearly found it amusing.

To show he was just a regular guy Father Norm told a joke. A priest was out golfing and it began storming. On the fourteenth hole he was swinging his five iron for a shot to the green when he was struck by lightning. When his playing partners arrived there was no sign of him or his clubs. The priest had vanished.

In heaven, with St. Peter, the priest was crying his eyes out. "Be happy my son, you are in heaven with God. We know how much you enjoy golf so with special permission I had your clubs make the trip as well. You will be able to play all of our courses with your own equipment."

The priest was inconsolable and continued his sobbing. "I know that you felt there was more for you to do but this is God's will." The wailing continued. "Are you so upset because of all the friends you have left behind?"

The priest shook his head 'no' and continued his lament.

"Why are you so distraught then?"

"I left my pitching wedge on the thirteenth green."

One piece of advice the minister gave me when the round was over. "If you're ever out golfing and it begins to thunder and lightning go to your bag and hold a 1-iron high in the air."

"Why would I do that?"

He looked at me with a twinkle in his eye. "Son, not even God can hit a 1-iron."

The priest had some solemn words for me as well. "Quoting Ben Hogan 'may thy ball lie in green pastures, and not in still waters.'"

When the eighteen holes were in the books none of us had the perfect round but we did have some fun. They were just regular guys. I did notice that the cars the priest and minister drove were just as nice as their golf gear. Anyone who decides to try and help the rest of us get to our final reward is a super-hero to me and deserves a special treat now and then.

Reason eight that golf is better than sex:
Doing it by yourself will not cause you to go blind.

HOLE NINE
The Rider

Proper golf etiquette is clear on the issue of appropriate language while in mixed company. Don't say anything you wouldn't say if your mother was standing there. My mother used a bar of soap to make sure my brother and I kept our mouth in check. I try to remember that at all times.

WHILE THIS FRONT NINE is almost in the books there is one group of people I want to make sure I recognize. Those are the friends, usually wives, that ride along in the golf cart for the expressed purpose of keeping their partner company and providing moral support. This takes a very special person. They usually don't play golf and may not even like it, but they spend four plus hours sitting in a golf cart just to make someone else happy.

Usually, but not always, it is a wife or girlfriend as the ride along. This is actually so common that most courses have a rate just for observers. This topic is being covered on the ninth hole because this is where the ride along frequently ends. Sometimes amiably, sometimes not. **[A wife watched her husband rake the green and replace divots then commented. 'I can't even get him to put his dishes in the sink.']**

For the purposes of illustration I will use the ninth hole at Heritage Golf Course in Johnson County, Kansas. The ninth hole is a par five with a ninety degree dogleg right. From the dogleg it's still over two hundred yards to the green.

A couple of years ago I was teamed with a man and his wife; she was ride along number one. Then there was a woman and her older sister. The older sister was another ride along. Even though there were six of us there were only four golfers. After eight holes the wife was getting tired and a bit cranky.

"I've been up since six and watched you play half the course. I'm ready to go shopping." We were waiting our turn to tee off for the last hole on the front nine. The group ahead of us was still in the fairway. **[I find it much easier to get up for a six o'clock tee time than ten o'clock for church.]**

"I told you this would be four hours or more. Besides I'm doing really well. I have two birdies. You're my luck charm." He was being sincere. Par-Man actually hoped she stayed because he had a chance to shoot par or better.

"She looked at him and asked. "How many birdies can you get?"

"Well, eighteen I guess."

"Looking at him lovingly she replied. "You poor dear, why is it you only have two?"

It was agreed that she would be leaving us at the turn she would go shopping and return in two and a half hours to pick him up. I don't know if she really thought two birdies were really pathetic or if she was being really clever. Whatever she was thinking, her end goal, shopping at the mall, was achieved.

In the other cart the lady who was golfing, and quite proficiently I might add, really wanted her sister to leave. This golfer and her ride along were facing the reverse situation. The rest of us knew at the first hole this was a mistake.

It turned out that the rider was also a golfer but had had some surgery done on her foot and couldn't play. But she could offer advice. She offered advice to all of us, even though none of us wanted it. **[There are two things you can always count on: one, the worse the golfer the more likely he will be to give you advice, two any golfer who claims he doesn't cheat also lies.]**

For eight holes my cart partner, Darren, I forget the other names since my system for instant recall of players names had not been perfected for five names, was a very quiet man. On the sixth hole, a long and difficult par three over a small ravine, he remained silent even when his ball ended up down in the ditch, unhittable.

The sister with the bad foot was coaching the sister who was golfing: Now keep your head down and swing through the ball. What club do you have? You know you have a tendency to overestimate how far you can hit it. The wind is across so aim left. This is only the sixth hole so let's not get behind early.

The sister who was the Golfer: Thanks. I got this, just sit back and relax.

Bad Foot: You have a really good round going I'd like to see if you can beat my best score.

Golfer: I beat it last spring in Orlando at that Disney course.

Bad Foot: Not really. That course was much easier than the course where I shot my seventy-five.

Golfer: Whatever helps you sleep at night.

Finally she teed it up and hit a nice shot right onto the green.

Bad Foot: If you had aimed left that would be in birdie range.

Golfer: It's on the green so by definition it's already in birdie range.

Bad Foot: Yeah, I suppose, but long putts aren't your strength.

And so it went. Now it sounds much worse than it really was. They both gave as good as they got and Golfer took no pity on Bad Foot. They were also very civil, nothing snarky or vicious. While they didn't seem to be affected by the banter it was wearing on the rest of us.

As we waited to hit our tee shots on nine Golfer suggested, again, that Bad Foot go shopping, put her foot up, get her hair done or change the oil in her car, anything. Bad Foot either didn't get the hint or was so concerned that her sister might beat her score that she felt duty bound to stay.

Darren looked at me and asked. "You think if I gave her my credit card she'd go shopping with the wife? Then they could both come back together." **[Golf and marriage are very similar. To be good at both you have to work at it and they are both expensive.]**

"Don't know but it's worth a shot."

But on the golf course things have a way of sorting themselves out. Whether it's the mysterious golf gods or nature needing to be in balance, things tend to work out. Golfer hit a poor tee shot and needed two to get to the dogleg. Her third shot was errant right and in some tall grass. It took another shot for her to get out of jail, so her fourth shot to the green ended up short. By the time she chipped on she was laying five. A double bogey was probably the best she could salvage.

"Well it was a good round for eight holes. At five over on the front I'll never beat a seventy-five." Golfer wasn't all that upset as she analyzed her situation.

"I'm going shopping. It's getting hot and I can't watch you implode like this. See you in a couple of hours." Bad Foot left for destinations unknown.

Half way through the eighteen it was clear that no one, including Par-Man was going to achieve the ultimate goal. We would all be over par. Some further than others. It was interesting how the Golfer seemed to play relaxed even with the double bogey on nine. The husband, however, went the other way. Maybe he was worried about the wife burning up his credit card or maybe he really believed that she was good luck.

"Well, I had a forty one and you had a forty five." Darren looked at me and shrugged after I announced the scores. It didn't seem like his forty-one, a respectable total, was a big deal to him.

"I'm just happy to be here."

"What do you mean?" Par-Man was curious.

He looked a little sheepish but finally responded. "I spent a long time learning to play golf. I didn't want to get on the course unless I was sure that my performance would be up to par."

He laughed at his joke. I smiled. "How long have you been learning to play?"

"I started taking lessons five years ago. I studied putting, chipping, short irons, long irons the rules, everything. I spent so much time trying to be perfect that I forgot to enjoy myself. Turns out you can't study or practice having fun." Darren was grinning as he spoke.

"So what finally got you on the course?"

"My daughter wanted to quit dance class because she wasn't getting any better. I gave her this great speech about living in the moment and enjoying the trip. She took me in the garage and pointed at my golf clubs and said, 'show me.' So about three weeks ago I started enjoying the journey. Turns out I'm such a lousy golfer that the journey and people are the only part that I will ever be able to enjoy. I intend to do just that."

"I understand. Believe me I do. Golfing is the most fun I have with my clothes on." We both laughed.

A little known rule is that the player is the sole judge if his lie is unplayable or not. Sometimes taking an unplayable lie and following the line of relief could save a stroke. It's something to keep in mind.

Turned out that Darren was fairly philosophical, back on the sixth hole after he hit his tee shot into the ravine, he commented on his last three shots. "Everybody knows that bad shots come in groups of three and that was my third. The cycle has ended." Then, his wedge shot into the green after the drop and penalty shot went off the hosel and into the sand. "Look at that. I just started a new cycle."

Reason nine that golf is better than sex:
On the course, a sub-par performance is a good thing.

THE TURN

Proper golf etiquette suggests that if you have invited someone to join you for a fun afternoon on the links and he is already behind by eight strokes you should offer to buy the beer. Unless he's behind one stroke for each beer he's already had.

THIS IS A TRADITION LIKE NO OTHER. Curling and bowling are the only other two major sports where you can play the game and drink beer at the same time. Because of this and because almost anyone can get into golf there are those that don't consider it a sport. They would be wrong.

Just like curling and bowling simply participating is easy. Getting to the point where you can achieve the goal of par is a life-long pursuit. Most golfers, over 98% who play the game, never shoot a round at par or below and never get a hole-in-one. Getting into the sport is simple, doing well is extremely difficult.

The point to the Turn is to regroup. There's a saying, 'now we start a new nine.' It's a second chance on the same day. Everyone refers to their scores by saying what they had on the front nine then the back nine. Handicaps can be calculated on a per nine hole basis. When you do that the two nines, when you play eighteen, are calculated independently. Bets are made based on the two nines independently. A Nassau bets both nines separately and then the combined score.

Most people have heard the story that it takes eighteen shots to finish a bottle of Scotch at one shot per hole and that's why there are eighteen holes. Untrue. St. Andrews in Scotland set the number of holes at 18 in the late 1800's up until then a course could have had anywhere from 12 to 23 holes and many did.

Making the Turn became popular when courses allowed players to start on 10 and play to 18 first. Others would play 1 through 9. They all met at the clubhouse, at the Turn. On a few occasions this is where I have lost some of my playing partners.

Every once in a while someone in the group had only planned on playing nine but usually it's outside forces that conspire to cut the round short. I've heard them all but there are two major categories. Either the golfer in question has reached the limits of his patience after a particularly bad front nine or the little woman only signed off on a two hour kitchen pass.

Once, a playing partner used the USGA to add nine holes. On the third hole, a short par three the second person to tee off, Tommy, aced it. The hole was up on a hill so we didn't see it go in but when we got to the green there was no ball to be found. It had decided to hide in the cup. Tommy was understandably excited. As the remaining six holes played out my friend was having a once in a lifetime round. At the turn he called the missus and told her he had to play the remaining nine otherwise his ace would not count. **[The longest recorded hole in one occurred in March 1961 when Lou Kretlow aced the 16th hole at Lake Hefner Golf Course in Oklahoma City. The hole was 427 yards long.]**

The wife extended the kitchen pass for another few hours. A third member of our foursome offered some clarification. "The USGA recognizes a hole in one for nine holes. As a matter of fact if you are playing in a match and the match ends before nine holes then the hole in one still counts. The fact is an ace struck in a scramble counts."

Tommy looked at the rules policeman and said, "Let's keep that our little secret."

It has always amazed me how good a hotdog at the turn tastes, it's like having one at a baseball game. Maybe it's because you're hungry or maybe it's being outdoors. The other thing that is very satisfying, especially on a hot day, is an ice cold beer or soda. Golf courses want to help all of us watch our calorie intake. That is the only reason I can think of for them to keep concession prices so high and prohibit golfers from bringing their own supplies (a pet peeve of Par-Man's).

Refreshed, hunger satisfied and a brief rest, now to attack the second nine holes, referred to as the back nine.

The Back Nine

HOLE TEN
CELIA

Proper golf etiquette says that when the starter adds someone new to your group that you welcome them by introducing yourself and your playing partners. Remember one day you may be the someone new.

STARTING THE SECOND NINE is like spring, a season of hope. Something to drink and eat, a few moments of peace and quiet and then head to the tenth hole. As is usually the case the group ahead of mine took a lot longer dawdling in the clubhouse and they haven't even teed off yet. If it's hot then I will be in the furnace longer. If it's cold then I'll be in the icebox for an extended period. If it's a beautiful day and the weather is perfect then the group ahead of mine teed off a few minutes ago and we are the ones holding things up.

For Par-Man the tenth hole is often like the first hole. Why? Because every once in a while the group changes. If there is room, another player might be added, especially if they are only playing nine. I've had a dozen or more instances where this has happened. One sticks out more than the others.

"I'm Ernie; the starter said I should team up with you gentlemen. I hope that's all right?"

Two things need to be explained. I didn't need to devise a way to remember Ernie's name. I already had the names of the others in my group committed to memory so I would have no problem recalling 'what's his name.' Second, being polite Ernie asked permission to join our group. The common practice is to accept the single. But not always.

Several years ago, that's how long ago it has been since being rejected by a group, I was told I was not welcomed to join the threesome the starter had assigned me to. How do I know? That was the easy part.

"Good morning. The starter said I should team up with you…"

"He did, did he?" *The shortest member of the trio in front of me was obviously the leader.*

Stomping off toward the starters shack, an oasis of sovereignty, the man demanded an explanation.

"Why are you saddling us with a player we didn't invite?"

"What?"

"We don't want you adding to our group. I booked the tee time for myself and my friends. No one else is invited."

The starter was clearly taken aback. Golf protocol is clear on the subject. The starter runs the tee box and having strangers join groups that are less than full on busy days is standard practice.

"Listen, we're really packed today and it is our policy…"

"I don't care what you do with everyone else but I want my group left alone." *The words sound harsh but the man was actually being very civil to the starter.*

It was not reciprocal. "I don't care who you are or what you want. You're a threesome and I'm making you a foursome. Now, you're up."

The short man turned. There were daggers coming out of his eyes, they were directed at me. This was going to be a miserable round, even though I was only planning on playing nine. The next two and a half hours would be awful. I did the only thing I could. Walking up to the starter I told him that I was willing to wait and go with another group. "Listen, your life and my life will be much better if we just let them go off as a threesome."

"I know but I hate giving into them."

"Sometimes discretion is the better part of valor." *I just didn't want the hassle. This kind of thing just ruins a round.*

"Sit tight." *The starter called the clubhouse and after a couple of minutes the club pro appeared. After talking to the starter he walked down to the tee box and spoke to the threesome. It was a one way conversation.*

In the end I waited less than twenty minutes and was put with a new group and I was given a voucher for a free round.

Back to the current situation. What's his name, Ernie, seemed nice enough and wasn't all yappy. As a show of respect he teed off last on ten. At Minor Golf Course, just across the state line in Missouri, the tenth hole is a par four dogleg right. It's not a very hard hole as long your tee shot is placed so that there is a shot to the green. Ernie's tee shot was placed perfectly. It was a hundred yards to the green, a baby wedge for most people. That's when the three of us found out Ernie was just a bit strange.

Ernie had out driven all of us but instead of waiting for those behind him to hit he walked right up to his ball. "Ernie, watch out!" I was ignored.

Without regard for our shouts he marched up to his ball, swung and hit his ball on to the tenth green. It was a fine shot just fifteen feet from the pin. Ernie then proceeded to the green and putted out. We stood there astounded at his disregard for normal golf protocol.

After parring the hole Ernie simply walked to the next tee. We never saw him again. Maybe he was trying to break Richard Lewis' record. **[Lewis played 11,000 holes in 2010, all at the Four Seasons Resort and Club in Irving, Texas. A documented record.]**

On another occasion my cart partner and I were paired with two people, a young man and his girlfriend. The introductions were a tipoff as to how the next nine holes were going to be. "I'm E. J. and this is Chester." (Yes, that was his name.)

"I'm Harold." That was all he said. He didn't make any attempt to introduce his playing partner. After an awkward moment Chester walked over and introduced himself to the young lady.

"My name is Celia." That was all she said.

I noticed that while there were two sets of clubs the ones behind the driver, Harold, looked like something you might get at a garage sale. The ones behind the passenger, Celia, were Callaway's, nice ones.

There was no further conversation; it was our turn to tee off. Chester and I were playing the white tees. After two pretty good shots we waited for Harold. His tee shot was, well, pathetic. I got in the cart and Chester and I moved up to the red tees for Celia. She walked up and launched a drive that waved at all three of ours as it sailed past.

Her smile disappeared when Harold said, "Come on. Let's get going." He was a real jackass. Chester and I looked at each other and shook our heads.

Harold was short off the tee so he was going to hit first. Chester said to me, "Pull up next to Celia and walk her down to her ball."

She was long but somewhat left and we could walk to her ball without being in Harold's way. "Uh, okay."

I don't think I mentioned that Chester was about six-six and at least two hundred and fifty pounds. To increase the intimidating effect he was covered in tattoos. I had learned that while he looked like a gang-banger he was actually ex-special forces, Army.

I found out later, after Harold got much nicer to be around, that Harold's conversation with Chester went something like this.

Chester: Celia reminds me a lot of my younger sister. I loved her very much and was at her side when she died.

Harold: I'm sorry to hear that. I mean about your sister.

Chester: It really upsets me when you are mean to Celia.

Harold: I'm not being mean. I just don't like to golf but she loves it.

Chester: She looks like she's pretty good.

Harold: Yeah, she beats me every time.

Chester: This time when she beats you she will enjoy it because you compliment her every single time she hits a good shot or sinks a putt.

"I then put my hand on his scrawny shoulder and asked him if he understood." Chester smiled. "He said he understood."

The last half of the tenth hole and the remaining eight holes were a lot of fun for all of us, including Harold. Celia was good, not great, but certainly above average. On different holes she beat all of us guys. True to his word Harold was nice. After several holes he didn't seem to be forcing it, he was actually being nice.

"You did good Chester." Maybe Chester was a super hero in training?

He smiled, winked and got in his car. Before he left I motioned for him to stop. "Hey, by the way, I really am sorry about your sister."

"I never had a sister." He grinned broadly and drove away. Par-Man never saw Chester, Harold or Celia again. Such is the fate of the single golfer.

Par-Man failed that day as well. No one achieved par or better. We did play the back nine in record time, even with a woman in the group. **[Alice Miller set the record for an LPGA Tournament when she completed the 1997 Welch's/Circle K Championship in 1 hour, 26 minutes and 44seconds.]**

Something to keep in mind, your game and the game of your playing partners will improve in direct proportion to how polite you are to others. It has always been a source of wonder that good golfers forget they were bad golfers once. None of us come out of the womb able to hit it straight.

Reason Ten that golf is better than sex:
You can watch golf on TV without having to subscribe to a premium cable channel. Best of all you don't have to hide from your wife and kids while you watch.

HOLE ELEVEN
THE PRO

Proper golf etiquette says you should remind your playing partner to remark his ball if he moved it a club head left so his mark would not be in your way. You see the pros do it all the time. It would be uncouth to win a hole on such a small technicality. Wouldn't it?

"HEY, IT'S ME, CHRISTOPHER."

"Great to hear from you. What's up?" Christopher is a friend of Par-Man's that lives in Phoenix.

"Have I got a deal for you."

Christopher explained that he is friends with the professional golfer Dan Pohl. Christopher had arranged for a friend, Roger, and I to play a round of golf with Dan and he at the National Golf Club outside Kansas City. This is a Tom Watson course and the nicest course Par-Man had ever had the privilege of playing.

The day we arrived to play they were starting everyone on ten, not one. So two became our eleven, hence its location in this first volume.

When we were all together Christopher handled the introductions. "E. J. this is Dan."

"Very nice to meet you." I said as I extended my hand. Dan Pohl is sixty-one, about five eleven and in really good shape. I was jealous right away; Dan has a full head of hair.

"Looks like you need a new set of sticks." Those were his first words to me. He smiled and shook my hand firmly. I looked at my clubs and he was right.

Before we go any further Par-Man needs to point out that this was the biggest thrill of his twenty-five years in golf. The next few paragraphs will help you understand why this was so exciting.

Turning pro in 1977 Dan joined the PGA Tour a year later. He won two tournaments on the PGA Tour in 1986, when he finished fifth on the money list: the Colonial National Invitational and the NEC World Series of Golf. Dan's career includes 70 top-10 finishes and more than a dozen second or third place finishes. In 1987 he posted the lowest scoring average on the PGA Tour and won the Vardon Trophy. In 1988 physical injuries dramatically altered his competitiveness.

In major tournaments his best finish in a major was 2nd at the 1982 Masters Tournament which he lost to Craig Stadler in a playoff. He also had a third place finish at the 1981 PGA Championship and a T-3 at the 1982 U.S. Open.

In 1980 Dan led the tour in driving average at 274.1 yards, and again in 1981 with a 280.1 yard average. He was a member of the 1987 Ryder Cup Team. He was inducted into the Michigan Golf Hall of Fame in May 2004.

Since turning 50 in April 2005, Pohl has played on the Champions Tour. His best finish at this level has been a T-3 at the 2005 Commerce Bank Long Island Classic. Dan has served as an on-course TV golf analyst for NBC Sports working with Dick Enberg and Johnny Miller along with Roger Maltbie and others for several years. He lives in Phoenix, Arizona and enjoys hunting and fishing. He has a regular weekly radio show in Phoenix, "Arizona Golf" and is involved with Hopkins Golf as an executive in a golf club company founded by Greg Hopkins, the former CEO of Cleveland Golf.

[Jack Nicklaus, in 1963 became the youngest golfer to win The Masters. When he won again in 1986 he became the oldest.]

At The National the hole we played as number eleven is a par five that parallels a creek for almost three hundred yards and then turns left. The green is about two hundred yards away. Par-Man hit one of his best drives. It was straight and long. The other members of the group teed off and Dan was last.

"Wow, nice hit." Yet again I was amazed at how far Dan could hit the ball.

On an earlier hole he had impressed me beyond belief. Dan said, "If I get after this one and hit it on the left side there it will bounce onto the green." He aimed, addressed the ball and hit it exactly as he had predicted. On an ordinary par three that would be impressive but this was a par *four*. His tee shot was well over three hundred yards. To say I was impressed would be an understatement.

On this par five I stood by my ball and considered going for the green. Dan was eighty yards ahead of me. I decided to take a picture. When I tried to take the picture I had to reposition the angle of the shot. Dan was so far ahead of me that he was hard to see. I had him wave his arms so he could be seen in the distance. I have shown that picture dozens of times.

Meanwhile back on hole eleven Par-Man's second shot was short and a little off line, but hey, it was a par five. Dan was on in two.

"Boy, I wish I could do that." Par-Man's jealousy was showing through.

"Wishing has nothing to do with it. You can hit the ball the same way I do if you want to practice eight to ten hours a day, hit several hundred balls and listen to someone who knows more than you do." He looked at me. "That's what I had to do for years."

"Then you have to be able to deal with the mental side of the game." Dan looked at me, but I understood exactly what he meant.

Several years ago I was vacationing in Buffalo, Wyoming, a small town that helps support the hunting and fishing that draws tourists from all over the world. The family was there and they all went horseback riding. Par-Man is not equine friendly.

Well, one afternoon I went to the only golf course in town. When I pulled in the parking lot there were only three cars in it. Entering the pro shop I asked how much the green fee was.

"You a member?"

"No, I'm here on vacation and thought I'd get eighteen in before dinner."

"Okay, if you'll let me join you I'll take you out as my guest and you'll get the member rate." The person behind the desk was about twenty-five and looked bored to tears.

"Sure I'd love to have the company. But what will you do if someone else shows up to play?"

He took a cigar box from under the counter and placed it on the glass top. "They'll put their money in here." You gotta love small towns.

I paid the twenty-three dollars, the member rate, and took a cart out to my car to retrieve my clubs. I met the attendant, Joshua, at the first tee.

Turns out the kid was on the University of Minnesota golf team and had won several tournaments in Minnesota, where he went to school, and Wyoming, where he lived. He was a terrific golfer. On one hole I hit an eight iron on to the green just under thirty feet from the pin. Joshua hit his ball about eight feet away.

"What did you hit?"

"A seven iron."

"I hit an eight. Why did you have to hit one more club than I did?" My thought process was simple. He was the pro, sort of; he should be hitting shorter clubs than me, not longer.

He laughed and dropped two more balls where we were standing. He took an eight and nine iron, he showed them to me for emphasis, and hit them even closer to the pin. "Sometimes I just hit something different to see if I can do it."

Finally, about the eleventh hole, I asked why he was in Buffalo, Wyoming instead of on the tour. He laughed. "It's my brain. I can't deal with the pressure and I never practiced enough. I'm just not mentally disciplined."

When I met Dan Pohl, the PGA pro, at the National those words that Joshua said several years earlier came back to me.

[ESPN analyzed the major sports and decided that golf was the easiest sport for someone to get into and the hardest to master.]

When Joshua and I finished I was still in awe of his skill. On one hole he said, "I need to hit this into the side of the hill by the green, let the ball pop up and it will land on the green, then funnel down toward the pin. The shot was exactly as described, oh, by the way he was 210 yards out. Like a maestro conducting an orchestra he knew exactly what he wanted to accomplish. When I commented on his prowess he said. "The difference between a pro and someone like me is the difference between lightning and the lightning bug." He was right.

"By the way, how much did the member rate save me?"

"Two bucks."

"What does a membership cost?"

"Ten bucks for the season and you can keep your own cart at the course."

Like I said, you gotta love small towns.

During my eighteen holes with Dan Pohl he gave me several tips. Putting, driving, stance and chipping were all covered. When the round ended he offered some sage advice. "Changes made while playing a round will last a maximum of three holes to a minimum of not at all. If you don't practice nothing will take."

I have forgotten some of the pointers but not the advice. By the way Dan, my putting is better thanks to your tip.

Reason eleven that golf is better than sex:
When your equipment wears out, you can replace it.

HOLE TWELVE
The Gambler

Proper golf etiquette mandates that you compliment your competitor when he makes a good shot even if it might cost you some dough. It's a gentleman's game and a true gentleman smiles in the face of disaster. Besides, just maybe, you can get into his head if he thinks that three footer he just sunk was somehow difficult but he didn't see the danger.

UNLIKE HOLES ONE THROUGH ELEVEN — where the layout, design, degree of difficulty or the distance of the hole itself were part of the story — these factors have nothing to do with the story of hole number twelve. I knew there was going to be trouble from the beginning. Gambling and golfing go hand in hand but all the players need to be on the same page as to how serious these wagers are going to be.

It started on the first hole. One of the guys had a really nice chip and was about a foot and a half away. You know, that range where it might be a gimme or it might not. The man who hit the shot walked up and looking around, but at no one in particular, asked the others in the group, "Good?"

"It's good," was the reply from behind him. It was Jon who granted the gimme request.

The player who had chipped the ball, Dave, scooped it up with the back side of his putter.

"Hey, you can't do that! You're his partner." Rob was just a tad upset.

Jon replied. "Sorry, I forgot."

"Sure you did."

The gimme stood and we moved on. There was friendly banter back and forth among the four of them. I should mention that I was put with them as a fifth and wasn't involved in any of the high stakes betting.

Dave, Rob, Jon and Pat were all friends and had a regular Saturday tee time. This was Sunday though. It had rained all day Saturday and they all agreed to move their round out a day. The course was still wet and it was cart path only. Due to the conditions all four of them had been playing it up, wiping off the mud and moving the ball out of casual water. None of this was strictly by the rules. **[The first set of rules for golf was drawn up in Edinburgh, Scotland by The Gentlemen Golfers of Leith. The rules were single sentences numbered one to thirteen.]**

As previously mentioned Par-Man is not much of a gambler when it comes to golf. These four were betting on everything. By the third hole I was curious as to what the breadth of their gaming was.

"I don't want to be part of it but could you explain what you are betting on?" The answer was a lot more than I expected.

Pat, the one who was the most fastidious about the rules, answered. "The longest drive is worth a point, the first one on the green gets a point, the first one to sink his putt gets a point, the longest putt on each hole gets a point and if it's a sandie par then you get double points." **[A sandie is a par or birdie where the ball was in a sand trap at some point. A double sandie is where the golfer was in two traps. Though rare Par-Man has seen double sandie birdies on par fives.]**

"We are also playing skins that carry over. Oh, and we are not using any handicaps." Unless these guys were evenly matched this could end up very expensive for someone.

On the fifth hole I found out each point was a dollar. Dave had hit a good drive, he was long, and the other three all missed the green with their second shots. Dave hit the green and was away. He sunk a thirty footer and won four points from the other three. That was when the pot started boiling.

Dave was not a gracious winner. "I should have you guys pay up now. I don't want any of you cutting out."

Now I thought he was trying to be cute, but Jon took umbrage with the snide comment. "Bullshit, you have never been stiffed because you hardly ever win anything. Just keep your mouth shut."

There was some bite to Jon's words. Rob spoke up before this got really ugly. "Hey, relax, both of you. Let's play some golf. Who's up?"

The tension lessened and then, over the next few holes seemed to have disappeared altogether. However, on the back nine they initiated a new bet, one I had never heard of and had to be explained to me using small words. Rob took on the task of explaining this new game.

"We split up into two, two man teams. At the end of the hole we add the scores. But a 4 and 5 become 45 not 9. If the other team got a 5 and 6 then their score is 56. The winning team gets the difference or 11 points. Each point is worth a dollar. We switch partners every hole by putting the high and low scores together." As he explained it to me I realized how complicated their betting systems were. I found out later this was referred to as a Las Vegas bet.

Betting and golf go together. Several years ago a guy I know that is a groundskeeper, Chris, was notorious for his willingness to bet on anything. I was put in a group on a Sunday morning with Chris and another groundskeeper. The twelfth hole had a lake off to the left and really didn't come into play.

On the tee box the Chris said to his playing partner, "I'll bet you ten bucks that you can't hit a ball into the lake and scare those ducks away. If you get even one of them to fly off you win the bet. I'll give you three shots to get them airborne."

The lake was only a couple of hundred yards away and there were four ducks so the man took the bet. "You're on."

Teeing up the first shot hit at the far end of the lake, forty yards away and had no effect on the contented ducks. Again he teed up and this time the shot was on target and splashed down within ten yards of the first duck. Nothing happened. "What the hell! Those damn ducks must be blind."

"This is your last shot. Want to press?" A press in this instance amounted to a double or nothing wager.

Without hesitation the man replied. "You bet. I'm zeroed in now."

"Okay. Let's make the bet a per duck bet. If you get two to fly away I owe you double. But you owe me twenty for every duck that doesn't fly away." Chris was too sure of himself.

Par-Man had to step in. "We're up. We need to tee off or we'll be holding up everyone."

Looking behind us the group on eleven was finished putting. Chris had honors so he teed off and hit a long drive just left of center. I was next and hit the fairway but thirty yards short of Chris. The man who owed Chris ten bucks was up next.

Suddenly the man shifted his position. Looking at Chris he said, "You're on." Aiming at the lake he launched a shot that looked like a guided missile and was headed right at the four ducks. Depositing itself right in the middle of the four fowl.

"Son-of-a-bitch!" The man was incensed. Not a single duck budged.

Chris said nothing until the hole ended and then reminded his friend that he owed him eighty dollars. There was a thick tension for the rest of the round.

I heard later that Chris never made his associate pay up. He felt bad because he had gotten to the course early and set four decoys in the water. The bet was rigged from the get-go.

Now, back to Dave, Rob, Jon and Pat and their complicated betting system. Things came to a head on the twelfth hole. Dave and Rob were partners for their Las Vegas bet but they were on their own when it came to the bets they had set-up on the front nine, the individual bets, the long drive, first on, etc.

It was almost too complicated to understand. Rob was the furthest from the hole and no one was on the green, yet. Rob was also the best putter. He chipped on and ended up about eight feet away. Everyone else then chipped on. In the end Rob was first on, first in and was the only one to par the hole. He got three skins and two points. His partner, Dave, got a six but Jon and Pat had each gotten a six. That meant Jon and Pat owed twenty dollars (46-66) for the Las Vegas bet and Rob collected another pile of money for his eight foot putt.

Pat went nuts. "You played your ball up on the second shot."

"I did not!"

"Then you purposely hit your chip shot so that you could win first on and first in."

"You're crazy. If I was that good I wouldn't be out here with you guys."

Now Jon chimed in. "So now we're not good enough for you!" As he spoke Jon moved into Rob's personal space.

"You're going to welch on the bet aren't you?"

That was it. This was going to get ugly fast. I had to step in and calm everybody down. The solution came to me in a flash. "Hey, Rob you're up."

Pat and Jon looked at me like I was speaking another language. But it worked. **[The story is Phil Mickelson made a side bet with another pro on a practice round at the British Open. Phil won nearly a thousand dollars but made the loser pay off in pounds since they were in England.]**

The rest of the round was pretty mild. I didn't hang around to see who won what but Rob was smiling broadly and Pat was pouting. I could guess who was getting what. This is why I limit my golf betting to a maximum of two dollars, well sometimes five, but I'll bet you ten bucks that I never go over that.

Lee Trevino once said that real pressure is betting five dollars when you only have two dollars in your pocket. I have yet to play with anyone who was good enough to make a living betting. I've played with some good golfers but good golfers can be beat if they bet with someone where the wager is more uncomfortable for the good golfer than the challenger. There are lots of stories about good golfers losing on the last few holes because the pressure of the wager was harder on them than their opponent. A word to the wise.

Reason twelve that golf is better than sex:
If you are doing well, the fun will last for four hours.

HOLE THIRTEEN
The Resident

Proper golf etiquette is to not only repair your divot on the green but also a second divot that some inconsiderate nincompoop left behind. Being able to repair a divot is a badge of honor. You hit the green firmly enough to leave a mark. Savor the moment.

IT WAS A BEAUTIFUL DAY. The sun was shining, it was early May and the temperature was in the mid-seventies. Par-Man had decided to go to Painted Hills in Kansas City. On a Thursday evening the course would be almost deserted and the twilight greens fee was only twenty bucks. If I played quickly I'd easily get nine in and maybe eighteen. Not only did I go to the course as a single but I was going to play as a single. There was no one else in the pro shop. I would have the course to myself.

"There are two groups ahead of you at holes three and four but if you go over to ten there isn't anyone making the turn and you'll get more holes in." Par-Man loves starters that are helpful.

"Thanks, I'll do that."

When I got to hole thirteen there was another single preparing to tee off. Sometimes, even though we were both singles, people don't want to pair up. Maybe they are going to practice something or maybe they just like the solitude. When your two best shots are the practice swing and the gimme some alone time helps keep the tension level in check.

He saw me approach and waved me up. "We can play together or I'll let you play through"

The green on this fairly short par three already had three balls on it. One was quite close to the hole.

"I appreciate that. I'll just tee off and be out of your way." I stuck the tee in the ground and placed the ball on it. Then, as is my habit, I backed up and standing behind the ball looked at my target and tried to visualize the shot.

"Have you played here before?"

"A few times." Actually Par-Man played Painted Hills regularly when his daughter lived in town. She liked the course. After she moved to Cleveland he played it less frequently.

"Well, with the pin position where it is if you hit a lofted shot and land on that mound to the right of the pin the ball will bounce sideways and roll down toward the flagstick. If you hit a low shot then land about ten yards short of the green. The ground there is pretty hard and you'll get a good bounce. Since the green slopes up the ball will stop quicker than you think."

The man was a veritable font of information.

"You must play here a fair amount."

"Every damn day."

"You really like this course?"

"I do but I also get to play here for free, except I have to pay for the cart."

This was a story Par-Man wanted to hear. "How do I get a deal like that?"

The man pointed behind us. There was a house in the middle of the golf course. I knew it was there and had been told that a groundskeeper or someone like that had owned it at one time. As I remembered the last time I was at Painted Hills the place was vacant.

"I bought place that about a year ago. Free golf was one of the side benefits."

"How did you end up deciding you wanted to live on a golf course?" I was naturally nosey and cautiously curious.

"I was down here visiting a friend and we came here to play. There was a 'for sale' sign in the yard and I found out it was going to be sold to the highest bidder. There were no inspections and only one showing. The deal was you turn in a bid for the place as is and see if you were accepted."

"You must have really wanted to live here to outbid everyone else." The house was okay, nothing special and a little hard to access since there was only a winding side road that could be used to get to the driveway.

The man laughed. "I did it on a dare. I was the only bidder and got it for the price of a used car."

The look on my face must have conveyed my disbelief.

"Really. I was retiring anyhow. I was a school teacher in Minnesota and wanted to get away from the horrible winters. I have no children and I'm not married. I love to golf, so why not?" Par-Man's bullshit meter was reading zero.

"I'm John."

"E. J." We shook hands.

Now back to the thirteenth hole. "You sure know a lot about this hole."

"I know a lot about all the holes. I've been playing this hole since you teed off on ten. You hit the ball anywhere near the green and I can tell you what it will do. Try me. Where are you going to hit it?" John was waiting for an answer.

Now Par-Man is reasonably good but hardly good enough to call his shot. Who does he think I am? Babe Ruth for God's sake. "I don't think I can tell you exactly where this will land."

"Well what are you going to aim for?"

Looking at the green I saw the flag was centered in the green and a little forward. As mentioned earlier it sloped up the deeper it went. It looked level but the area surrounding the green was high on the right and dropped off precipitously to the left. After surveying things for a minute I had reached a decision.

"I'm going to hit an eight iron and aim for the front right quadrant of the green and let the ball roll up the slope and left after it hits."

Before I could do anything John stepped in front of me, teed one up and hit it at the target I had described. He turned toward me and started speaking while the ball was still in flight. "It won't run up the slope. We're above the hole and the slope is more severe than it appears. The ball will run a little right, not left. The mounds on the right create an optical illusion as to which way the ball will move."

His shot was not exactly on target but it was close enough to show me that he was correct. The ball moved as he had predicted. **[Speaking of predictions Doug Ford told the press he would win The Masters in 1957, and he did. He also predicted a score of 283, which was exactly what he shot for a final score.]**

"How many times have you played this hole?"

"About thirty or so."

My expression said it all, that wasn't so many. Then he added, "Today."

This was one of those rare times when I didn't get even nine holes in. We played the par three thirteenth hole a dozen times. After a few times I hit two knocked down sevens to within easy birdie range. It was kind of fun.

Before dark we went over to his place and had a soft drink. Turned out he was like Par-Man and didn't drink alcohol very often. There was a small lake in front and a side yard that was actually quite large. He had made a good buy.

I ran into John a couple of years later when I went to Painted Hills with some friends. He told me he had aced the thirteenth hole twice since our encounter.

Reason thirteen that golf is better than sex:
Your technique isn't nearly as important as results. The lower your score, the better you did.

HOLE FOURTEEN
THE OLD MAN

Proper golf etiquette precludes criticism. Even when someone hits a bad shot the best practice is to be silent. If you have to say something mentioning that it was well struck, the putt was on line or it had good direction are acceptable comments. Complimenting someone on the fact that they hit it a mile into the woods is inappropriate.

WHEN PAR-MAN FIRST PLAYED the next course it was called the Golf Club of Kansas City. Later it was bought out and renamed Canyon Farms Golf Club. Near the Lenexa, Kansas City Center this is one of the most challenging tracts in the area. We'll get to the hole itself in a moment but first a little about my group.

"My name is Austin and this is my brother Jordan. We are here visiting our uncle. He owns the largest trucking company in the state, Statewide Transport. I'm sure you've heard of it." In an instant I knew these two snooty guys were going to be difficult to be around for eighteen holes. They looked like the type that talk 70, dress 80 and, if lucky, shoot 90.

"I'm E. J. Nice to meet you." It wasn't but what else was I going to say.

The fourth member of our group was a decade older than Par-Man and looked like he had already played his best rounds.

Shaking hands with the three of us the elderly hacker said, "I'm George."

George was at least seventy, had a twenty year old set of clubs well-worn clothes and a hat that had been around since Jordan and Austin were in high school.

I played with an elderly gentleman once. He had no trouble seeing the ball he just couldn't remember where it went.

Unfortunately the round had been going as I expected. Jordan and Austin were spoiled brats, sophisticated brats, but spoiled none the less. They were pretty good golfers but talked down to the both of us in a passive aggressive way. More so to George, he just wasn't very long off the tee. **[For some people the only way they can increase the distance of their tee shot is to hit the ball and run backwards.]**

It should be noted that George made a bet with all of us on the first hole. It wasn't a real bet but more of a challenge. "I'll bet when the day is done I will shoot closer to my age than any of you." We all just sort of smiled. But when you think about it his proclamation made perfect sense.

The fourteenth hole par five is 551 yards and a slight dogleg right. All down the left side is a quarry wall that averages about sixty feet in height. It is difficult to lose a ball on this hole but it could get scuffed if you bounce it off the stone face. Jordan and Austin had visions of making it in two but both missed the green and had very difficult chip shots. Jordan had missed left and Austin missed right. I proved to be the exception to the rule and Par-man's second shot disappeared forever. **[Americans spend $600 million on golf balls every year.]**

Normally Par-Man really enjoys par fives. Even one that is 551 yards long is easily tamed with a good tee shot. Off the tee and 250 yards down the fairway the long par five is now a 300 yard par four. Hell, two seven irons and a one putt for birdie. It all seemed so simple. That had been my plan; it was a good plan.

The lost ball on the second shot had put a real kink in my strategy. George, however, was following his plan to the letter. I wanted to let him know I had noticed. "That was a nice tee shot, George."

"Thanks, but it's the next two that are really the important ones."

George was still a little over 320 yards out. But his next shot put him only a buck sixty out. "When I was younger I'd have been on in two." George's comment reminded me of a time my brother and I were out golfing with our dad.

We were playing a course dad had played when he was in his twenties. "You boys need to see what a real, old-time golf course layout is like."

It was a nice tract but other than domed greens it wasn't really any different than any other city course I'd played. Oh well, dad was happy and at his age all my brother and I wanted was for him to enjoy the afternoon.

On one of the holes my brother hit his tee shot long but errant. He was right behind a pine tree. The green was just the other side maybe an eight iron away, as long as the ball got high enough quickly enough. Don, my brother, decided he was going to punch it out and then chip up.

Dad coughed that attention getting cough. When we looked he said, "When I was your age it would be unthinkable to go around that tree."

I looked at Don and he shrugged. Repositioning himself it was clear the challenge was too much for him. Careful deliberation, smooth backswing and then the impact sound. He caught it flush and the ball took off like a rocket. Liftoff lasted a split second. The ball hit the tree bounced back and ended up about three feet from where it had just been struck.

"That's an impossible shot!" Don was pissed. "I don't believe you ever hit one over that tree."

Dad smiled slightly and responded. "First, I never said I hit one over that tree. But, it so happens I did, several times. Second, when I was your age that tree was only four feet tall."

Austin and Jordan chipped up and while they both were on the green they were in three putt range. I finally got on but I was laying five and not really in one putt range. George, on the other hand, was about six feet away after a beautiful third shot. George had hit two 160 yard shots perfectly.

"I'll bet you two a beer at the end of the round that E. J. and I will beat, not tie, the two of you on this hole when our scores are added together. You know, Vegas style." I looked at George. He smiled and his eyes shone brightly. "Don't worry I don't think they'll take the bet."

I knew what a Vegas style bet was but I don't think Austin and Jordan were listening. It was a sucker bet. There was no way they could win.

Of course as soon as he said that Austin spoke up. "You're on!"

To recap George and I were laying a total of eight and Austin and Jordan were laying six. Whether it was the bet or not, I'll never know, but my two opponents were nowhere close to tap-in or gimme range and it had taken each of them two putts to get there. **[Three putting a**

difficult green that is lightning fast and downhill is no reason to be embarrassed unless you had to use a wedge in between.] Even if they both parred the hole they would have a fifty-five. George, by sinking his six foot putt, would give us a forty something. It wouldn't matter what Par-Man did. I had no pressure, it was all on George.

I had not done any better. Like Austin and Jordan my first putt wasn't close. The green was fast and very undulating. That's how I saw it anyhow. No matter what happened Par-Man could not help or hurt his partner. **[Two things about putting and putters. One, never buy a new putter until you've had a chance to throw it and second chalant putts count the same as nonchalant ones.]**

Now it was up to George. Just as it appeared he was about ready to putt he stepped back. "You know, I'm not much of a beer drinker. If we don't beat you by ten points then the bet is off. That's a gift since your both laying four. All one of you has to do is par the hole. If we do beat you by ten or more then at the end of the round you have to clean our clubs. What do you say?"

"You can't possibly win by ten. What are you talking about?" Jordan wasn't being a jackass, this time. He was genuinely confused.

Par-Man decided that since I could help my partner at least I could explain the bet. "In a Vegas bet, the scores are not added arithmetically, they are simply placed one next to the other with the lower score first. If George and I get a five and seven respectively then our score is fifty-seven. If you and Austin get fives each then your score is fifty-five. Get it?"

They didn't answer immediately so George readdressed his ball and prepared to putt. "Fine. We'll take the bet." It was Austin again.

George smiled. "Done."

This was not a slam dunk. Even if George birdied the hole and I drained my putt we would have a forty-seven. If either Austin or Jordan sunk their putts then we would likely lose as they would get a fifty five at best and a fifty six on the outside.

George was six feet from the cup and he was away. He walked up and, you guessed it, drained that bad boy with no hesitation.

Whatever happened after George sunk his putt was going to decide the bet. My partner had done his part and now it was up to me, except

I wasn't out. Jordan was. Whether he was mad at Austin or just mad at the situation I'll never know but in an unexpected move he picked up his ball and conceded the hole.

Whether Jordan and Austin would have won was forever a mystery. The rest of the round was quiet and a little tense. But there was tension between Jordan and Austin. Unfortunately no one in our foursome achieved the goal of par or better.

To their credit Austin and Jordan cleaned our clubs and congratulated George again on his birdie. I walked out to my car and found out I was parked next to George. "That was a great putt. You must have ice water in your veins."

"The whole thing was stupid. I should have never made that bet. I was really lucky."

"Why did you make it then?"

"The jackass with the blond hair (Jordan) looked at my putt and just shook his head like there was no way I should be able to get that close. His arrogance made me mad."

"Maybe he was just admiring your shot." George glared at me as if to say, 'are you nuts.' "Well, maybe not."

I think of that encounter often. As it turned out George's prophecy was accurate, he shot closer to his age than any of us. I didn't find out until the end that he was eighty-two years young. He was only fourteen over his age. I wondered how many more birdies that old man had left in him.

Reason fourteen that golf is better than sex:
Even when you're eighty, you can always find a willing partner or two.

HOLE FIFTEEN
The Shot

Proper golf etiquette makes it every player's responsibility to keep a respectable pace of play. Normally being any further than one shot behind is considered slow. If someone from the group behind you comes up and offers you a replacement ball for the one you hit in the woods you can be pretty sure you're playing too slow.

"IF I HIT ONE OF MY BEST SHOTS, I can carry the tree, clear the water and end up close to the pin." How many times have we said or thought something like that? This was my dad's answer to that proclamation.

"If this has to be one of your best shots ever then ask yourself these questions before you swing. One, why would one of your best shots ever follow the shot that put you in your current predicament? Two, after I swing and the shot isn't what I wanted what is it I'll wish I had done? Third, is that what I should be doing? And finally, how many 'shots of a lifetime' are there? In the order the questions were asked the answers are usually, one: it won't, two: something else, three: then do something else now and finally: only one. By definition there can only be one shot of a lifetime. I can promise you, this isn't it."

On the fifteenth hole of this particular course I saw someone else's shot of a lifetime. It was a very warm and humid day in mid-August. Par-Man was with a congenial group. All three men were friendly and reasonably competent golfers. We were playing Shadow Glen in Olathe, Kansas. It was fifteen years ago and while I'm not a member, our corporate lawyer is, and he invited me out to play with some associates of his.

Now, the fifteenth hole at Shadow Glen is a par three and plays 176 yards. Long is really bad, a drop off into the woods. Right is covered by four sand traps and left rises up slightly and on that side there are two traps. Short is not a problem except that on a par three the tee shot is supposed to hit the really short grass not the fairway grass.

Unfortunately, Par-Man only remembers two of his playing partner's names. The lawyer was John and the man who hit the shot of a lifetime was Luther. The last member was an optometrist so we'll call him Doc, clever, huh? I saw this and I swear this is what really happened.

"You're up Doc." John was the unofficial honors watchdog.

It was a good shot, right at the pin. It took a couple of bounces and landed three feet to the left of the flagstick.

"E. J." I teed off and hit it short and right. I was still ten yards from the front edge of the green and twenty-five yards from the hole.

Now it was John's turn. He was long and likely in trouble. John shook his head and wandered back to join the rest of us. Now for the big moment.

Luther teed up and swung as hard as he could. The ball took off left and on a line. There was a reason Luther was hitting last.

"Oh, shit." Luther said it the way most of us say 'good morning.'

"That's going to be in the trees." John was a master of the obvious. The woods were left of the cart path which ran down the left side of the hole.

"Yeah." Luther saw what was happening.

About two thirds of the way to the hole the errant ball disappeared into the foliage. A second later there was a loud crack.

"Hit something." Again, the master of the obvious, John shook his head.

Then there was another crack, but different. The ball had been spit out and the golf gods thought it would be funny to have it bounce down the cart path.

"It came out." Doc was pointing in case anyone had not been paying attention. **[A regulation golf ball has 336 dimples however; all golf balls are not the same, the number of dimples ranges from 330 to 500 dimples. The most popular golf balls have between 380 and 432 dimples.]** This one now had a roguish cart path scar to go with those cute dimples.

The little white globe continued its trek through the universe of the cart path. While its trajectory had been altered by trees and asphalt, its end objective was being zeroed in on. The ball kept bouncing toward the green and the hole. The dimpled devil hopped toward the hole like a rabbit to safety.

That little thing had a lot of momentum. **[Momentum is mass times velocity in case you were interested.]** Careening along the cart path all of us watched. Closer and closer it got to the green. Then, after hitting the edge of the asphalt path, the ball kicked right and down the hill. It snuck between the two traps and ran on to the green.

Just like Louis Oosthuizen did on the 16th hole at the 2016 Masters, Luther's ball went toward Doc's. Luther's ball hit Doc's and that's where the similarity to Oosthuizen's shot ended. The 16th hole at The Masters is 181 yards. Oosthuizen's ball hit the one J. B. Holmes had already put on the green, ricocheted off of it and rolled in the cup for an ace.

Luther's ball hit Doc's and due to the fast green and slope nudged it and the ball started rolling toward the hole from the force of Luther's ball. **[Force is mass times acceleration, in case you had it confused with momentum.]** This is where you probably think one of the two balls made it to the cup. Nope. Neither ball made to the hole. But they were both really close.

"That was unbelievable!" John exclaimed.

"Look at that. You both have tap in birdies." Par-Man was astounded. That was the luckiest shot I had ever seen.

We approached the green and Doc and Luther both approached their balls in order to complete the tap in birdie. Luther, with the flagstick still in, tapped the ball which was only inches from the cup and in it rolled. Doc pulled the flagstick out and prepared to tap his in when a look of horror spread across his face. "You hit my ball!"

"What?" Luther was momentarily confused.

"They are both tap ins. What's the big deal?" John wasn't very interested in the whole thing but I could see that Doc was upset and getting more so by the second.

That became clear to everyone when Doc spoke. "His ball is not a tap in. He's 'outside the leather' by a foot. And my ball needs to be replaced to the spot where it was before he hit it. He gets penalized for hitting my ball, hitting the flagstick and putting the wrong ball. I get to put my ball back where it was without any penalty. I'll get a par for sure and maybe a birdie. He gets like a six or something."

Now you're thinking, why all the hubbub during a friendly game? I did not mention that the three of them had a variety of bets going. I'm not against a small wager but their wagers were not small, at least to me. I didn't pay that close of attention to everything they were betting on but by this time in the round Doc was down mid-three figures. He was the better golfer but somehow handicaps came into play. Luther was on the plus side of the wagering scale.

The bickering shifted into high gear in no time. To keep play moving it was decided to let the pro tell them the proper scores when the round was over.

Holes sixteen, seventeen and eighteen were uneventful. When they got to the clubhouse, the three of them made a bee line for the pro shop. I was at my car removing my golf shoes. Just as I was about to leave I saw them leave. None of them looked happy. I wanted to find out why.

Entering the clubhouse I saw the pro standing at the front window watching my playing partners leave. "Excuse me. I was in the foursome with John, Luther and Doc and saw what happened on the fifteenth hole. Would you mind explaining the rules to me?"

He looked at me and asked, "Which rule?"

"What do you mean?"

"Well, first off gambling by members is strictly prohibited." Then he winked. "That aside, the ball on the green that was struck needs to be replaced to its original position. The ball that came out of the woods and hit the ball already on the green is played where it comes to rest. Hitting the wrong ball is a two stroke penalty and you still have to hit your ball from wherever it was. The player whose ball you hit places his ball back where it was and there is no penalty to him. Hitting the flagstick on a putt from the green is a two stroke penalty. The player whose ball was on the green would have to mark the ball if asked or he could mark it on his own. It he wanted it marked he should have said so. Even if someone's ball hits your ball into the hole you have to replace it and play it from where it was. When neither of them did the proper thing they both lost the hole."

"I see." Then I asked the real question. "What did they decide?"

"I have no idea. They were going to discuss it outside."

As I drove home I realized that Doc's excellent shot that set him up for a possible birdie and Luther's horrible shot that also set him up for a birdie, in the end, cost them the hole. If they had just looked at the balls they both would have likely put twos on their scorecard and been quite happy whether they followed the rules exactly or not.

Reason fifteen that golf is better than sex:
You are allowed to have golf calendars on your office wall at work and tell golf jokes without worrying about the Human Resources people accusing you of harassment.

HOLE SIXTEEN
THE FIVER

Proper golf etiquette is to let faster groups play through. This speeds up the game, helps fast and slow players stay with a rhythm they are comfortable with and keeps you from getting hit by a golf ball, which really hurts.

THIS HOLE HAS TWO INTERESTING TIDBITS. One has nothing to do with the layout of the hole and the other has everything to do with the layout of the hole. Par-Man will cover the first situation, well, first.

At the sixteenth hole of Deer Creek the foursome that Par-Man was with prepared to tee off. **[The wooden tee was patented in 1899 by George Grant of Boston.]** Since the round had been fairly normal the names of the players have been lost, Par-Man's memory system hadn't been perfected yet. The only player of importance is the fellow who teed off last. We'll call him Bert.

Bert's drive was down the middle. He had been driving well all day. Actually, he had a good game overall. He was only teeing off last because we were playing ready-golf; we had no honors police in this group. **[The idea of honors was designed to put pressure on your playing partners. It was like saying 'top this.']**

Surprisingly we were all on the green in two. At Deer Creek the 16th hole is fairly short and is a good scoring opportunity even for a bunch of hackers. I don't actually remember where everyone's shots ended up but Bert was at the front of the green. Unfortunately for him the pin was at the back and it was a long but narrow green. Bert was at least ninety feet from a birdie.

As Bert stood over his putt he began to talk. He had done this throughout the round. We had all figured out that he wasn't talking to us and didn't really want a reply. It was a monologue as opposed to a conversation. "The last long putt I sank with this putter was when I bought it. Don't let me down now."

I should mention that on the first hole Bert was marking his ball. "Putting your mark on it so you can identify it?" Seemed like a logical question to Par-Man.

"No." He held up the ball so I could see it. There were ears and eyes drawn on it. My reaction was involuntary. I didn't mean to react like he was just a wee bit crazy.

"It's so it will listen and then go where it's supposed to." Oh, that cleared it up and made perfect sense. He was so serious I decided to simply walk away. I wondered if as he stood over this really long putt if he somehow believed that the ball could hear him and then be able to see the hole?

Bert's putt was solidly struck, it rolled over a knoll and then down the other side. But he had not allowed enough for the break and the ball rolled left and was still fifteen feet from its target. The rest of us putted in turn and now Bert was away again.

Needing to sink this for par Bert wasn't about to leave it short; and he didn't. When he hit it hard the ball rolled right through the break and stayed right of the hole. His ball stopped two feet past the cup.

We were all a little stunned when he bent over and just picked up his ball. He had been putting everything out, no gimmes. When he stuck the ball in his pocket, took his clubs off the cart his playing partner and he had been sharing, and started walking back toward the clubhouse we were all speechless.

Par-Man had to know what the hell was going on. "Bert, where are you going?"

"I reached my limit." That explained nothing.

"Limit of patience?"

He stopped and turned. Looking at me like I was dense, which is true sometimes but I didn't feel like that applied in this instance, he explained. "Every so often I give myself a target. I take the scorecard and write in what I believe I should get on each hole. I then add it up.

Today my target was seven over par or a 79. That second put was my 79th shot. I'm done."

"How often do you do this?"

"Eight to ten times a season."

"I've got to know; have you ever finished a round with that sort of approach?"

"Oh, yes. I'm successful two to three times a year. The key is to set a reasonable target. When I take this approach I sit down before the round and fill in what I think I should score on each hole. That becomes my par, so to speak. It actually is kind of fun and a real challenge. It also eliminates most of the pressure."

We wished each other well and I went to finish the last two holes. I told the rest of my group of the conversation with Bert and they didn't care one bit. Par-man wondered if he should change his target to something more reasonable than a round of par or better, no way.

Several years ago Hank Aaron was asked about his round of golf that he played celebrating the tenth anniversary of hitting his 715th home run. "It took seventeen years for me to reach 3000 hits as a major league baseball player. I'm half way there after one round of golf."

The second sixteenth hole encounter was all about the layout. It happens that this sixteenth hole is also a par three. The course was Falcon Ridge in Lenexa, Kansas. The layout of this par three is one of the most diabolical Par-Man has ever seen.

It's only about 160 yards but a lake runs the full length on the left side of the hole. The green actually juts out into the water so the fairway is not even as wide as the green. Long is wet or in the trees, right is across the cart path and into some heavy rough. Short is all right but then your laying two when you chip on.

Another feature of this hole is that the green has a stone retaining wall more than half way around the perimeter. The green is within a yard of the retaining wall. On this day the location of the flag was long and left, a real sucker location. The only safe play is right of the pin, and keep it a little short.

Now a little bit about the other three members of the foursome. Two of the members of our group were members at Falcon Ridge, Clint and Herb. The third member of the quartet was actually visiting from out of town. Here on business, something to do with Hallmark Cards, Charles had an afternoon to kill so he decided to golf.

Par-Man was up first and hit a 6-iron aiming for the middle to right side of the green. It made it on but just barely. It was on the front right portion of the green. Clint and Herb followed and were both on the green and like Par-Man they were well right, but safe. Charles was last and for a reason.

Maybe it was the rented clubs or maybe it was his herky-jerky swing. Whatever the reason he was not a good golfer, and that was being kind. But, to his credit, he played quickly and never once got mad. Falcon Ridge is laid out end to end. Fairways don't parallel each other so it is possible to be in trouble on either side of the fairway on almost every hole. Poor Charles had spent so much time in the woods he probably knew what vegetation was edible.

He had not faired too well on the par three's so far and this would be his last attempt at a par. All teed up he switched clubs at the last minute. "I think I'll need a little more club what with the wind and all."

We looked at each other in disbelief. The day was dead calm but, hey, whatever works. He addressed the ball and after standing motionless for several seconds swung, hard. The ball cracked as it made contact with his club face and shot straight at the pin. The line was perfect, the distance, not so much.

"That's going to be long." Clint commented.

"Real long." Herb echoed the problem.

It was a high arching shot that sailed over the flagstick and toward the water behind the green. A moment later it disappeared into the water. Unexpectedly there was a smack, loud but not like a ball hitting a cart path or like a ball splashing into the water. It was somewhere in between. Appearing in the clear blue sky the ball came out of the water and up to the green. It hit the flag stick near the flag and fell sideways, toward the damn water.

The ball hit the green and ran left. A second later the little white dot disappeared again, over the side of the green.

"Did you see that?" Charles was as happy as he could be. "That's the best shot I've ever hit!"

"The ball is in the water Charles." I didn't want to ruin his moment but I wasn't sure he had seen where the ball ended up.

"I know. I don't care. I can tell all my friends what happened. They won't believe me."

Clint looked at me and said. "I saw it and don't believe it."

"I guess I need to hit a second ball?" Charles wasn't sure what the rule was. He had hit several balls into hazards but always just dropped one where ever he wanted and hit again. Apparently he wanted to preserve the sanctity of the hole so he teed up and hit a second ball.

"Hit a provisional."

"Oh, okay." He teed up and prepared to flail away again.

Par-Man felt obliged to state the obvious. "Hit this one a little easier."

Charles nodded appreciatively and swung. It was right at the pin and again it looked to be long. The ball hit the flagstick and dropped straight down. The flagstick was vibrating as the ball disappeared into the hole.

"A hole in one!" Charles was going nuts. I looked at Clint then at Herb. Who was going to tell him? As unfair as it sounded it was just a par.
[Tiger Woods made his first hole in one at eight years old.]

Fortunately Charles realized it before we were forced to pee on his parade. As we rode to the green Charles was the happiest guy in the county. When we got to the green and walked up to the flag that all changed.

His first ball had not gone in the water. It was just off the fringe, buried in some tall rough. Charles was told that was the ball he needed to play. His provisional was just that, a provisional in case we couldn't find his first shot. "So I don't have a par?"

"No, but you could get a birdie."

"I'd rather have the par."

He finished with a five. I told you he was a terrible golfer.

The sixteenth reason that golf is better than sex:
Doing it with your family doesn't get you arrested or on the sex offenders' list.

HOLE SEVENTEEN
THE STRATEGIST

Proper golf etiquette is to leave the rake in the bunker. When not in the bunker the rake can interfere with a ball. We wouldn't want the rake to stop a ball headed for the trap, would we?

THIS HOLE, SEVENTEEN, has always carried a special significance for me. If I do well here and finish eighteen well then I feel like I have accomplished something. Think about it: if the round has gone horribly wrong this will right the ship for the next round. If the round is going well this is the way to complete a memorable eighteen holes.

The seventeenth hole at Swope Memorial Golf Course in Kansas City is one of Par-Man's favorite holes. At 550 yards it plays like a true par five. The tee boxes set behind an area of rough that makes the hole appear longer. Bending slightly left there is rough all the way across the fairway a hundred yards from the green. In front of the green on both sides are bunkers that are only ten yards apart and they angle away protecting the green from anything except a well placed third shot. Trying to run it up from afar is almost impossible.

This hole is here because the first time Par-Man played it was when the lesson of strategy and course management really sunk in. **[Swinging harder, to get a few more yards, will always cost you ten times what you planned to gain. If I could put this in double bold I would.]**

This particular group consisted of three others, two men and a woman. But let me first set the stage before we get into the reason this is the seventeenth hole picked for Volume One. We had just come off a lightning and rain delay. It only lasted about thirty minutes but the rain had come down in buckets for twenty of those thirty minutes. The wind had also picked up, but was calm now. The horn sounded and we got the all clear. It was time to tee off and resume play.

Having honors Brent teed off first. Brent was a good golfer and was only three over with two holes left. Par was his goal and he had actually done it several times before. Par-Man hoped this would be one of his few success stories. Par-Man doubted it though. In fact Par-man was convinced that Brent was closer to eight over par. **[One of the people Par-Man played with regularly was such a liar that the only time he got an ace he put zero on his scorecard.]**

We weren't wagering in any way and a motto I tried to adhere to was that once you pay your money you can play any way you want. Tee it up in the fairway; it has no impact on how I play. You want to call eight footers a gimme; again, that's your prerogative. This attitude helps keep peace on the links.

God and St. Peter were teeing off to play a round of golf. God, of course, was up first. Taking off like a rocket the ball went straight and then sliced left; God is left handed, into the trees. It rattles around and then drops right next to a squirrel. The little critter picks up the ball and starts to run across the fairway when an eagle swoops down and grabs the squirrel. Flying off the poor squirrel drops the ball, it falls on to the green and into the hole.

St. Peter looks at God and asks, "We going to play golf or are you going to screw around?"

Brent's tee shot was down the fairway but to the left side. He was still three hundred plus yards away from the green. Having the next best score I prepared to hit next. My drive was more towards the middle of the fairway but not as long as Brent's. **[The longest recorded drive on an ordinary course is one of 515 yards by**

Michael Hoke Austin of Los Angeles, California, in the US National Seniors Open Championship at Las Vegas, Nevada on September 25, 1974.]

Alice should have been next but because she was using the forward tees, for convenience, she always teed off last. Her grandfather, Orrin, was up next. He probably should have been using the same tees as Alice but the male ego being what it is he couldn't bring himself to move forward. In earlier conversation Orrin commented that he was nearly fanatical about golf. When he was younger he would play four or five times a week.

"If someone stuck a flag on top of Mount Everest I'd try and play there." Orrin had a good sense of humor. He took the game seriously but he never once got mad at the fact that his deteriorating skills were letting him down. Turns out he had been Alice's instructor.

She had said, "At first I found it very confusing: hit down to make the ball go up, swing left to go right, the person with the lowest score wins and usually the winner has to but the drinks. But when the mechanics were explained it made more sense." **[22.8% of all golfers are women.]**

As expected Orrin's shot off the tee went about a buck sixty. He seemed fine with that. Then he walked up to Alice and asked, "Okay, the weather has affected the course what is your strategy for this hole?"

I had seen them talking before we teed off on the first hole and periodically they would get together but this was the first time I was close enough to listen in.

"Well, if I hit my normal tee shot it will go one ninety and die right there because I hit a fairly high drive and the ground is now wet and soft. Even a good three wood for my second shot will still leave me about one forty out. (The tee box for the women had her at 480 yards tee to green.) But the pin is to the back so I'd really be one fifty-five or so. I have a 50/50 chance of getting my approach shot close with my six iron. I should figure on a chip on to the green and then if I two putt a six. If I can chip close or get my third shot on or one putt then I get par. The greens will be slow, now that they are wet and there may be some water or mud fly up when I hit my fairway shots." She went on with two or three more keys to success.

Orrin saw me and when they were done walked back in my direction. Alice prepared to tee off. "That was quite an analysis."

"I believe it's important to have a plan for the hole. Each shot needs to connect to the next one. You've seen it. Hitting long isn't always a good idea." He tilted his head toward Brent and said, "He hit it a long way but I'd rather have your shot any day. He can't reach the green and his angle to the pin is so severe that he has a good chance of ending up in that rough in front of the green. You're not as long but you have two choices: hit short of the rough and have a hundred and a half to the pin or hit over the rough and have a sand wedge to the pin." He wasn't done yet.

"I only have one option, lay up short of the rough. But, unlike Brent I have an easy shot because I have sixty yards left to right to work with." Alice hit and as she predicted the ball went just shy of two hundred yards and she was smack in the middle of the short grass.

Orrin appeared to be about seventy and he reminded me of the rich golfer who showed up one day with a beautiful twenty-five year old redhead on his arm. He introduced her to his friends at the country club as his wife. When she went to powder her nose his buddies gathered around and asked, "How did you get her to marry you?"

"I lied about my age."

"What? Did you tell her you were fifty-five?"

"No, I told her my golf score and age were the same, ninety. I was half right."

I watched as the hole unfolded just as Orrin had predicted. Alice got a six with a tap in and I parred it. Partially because I felt relaxed and confident. Orrin hit his third shot fat and he and Brent ended up with bogeys. Had Brent not sunk a twenty footer, his first one all day, he would have had a double because his second shot went into the rough.

When the round was over I stopped Orrin, "Thanks for the lesson. I'll put it to good use."

"You're welcome. Just remember a good plan is better than a good shot because a good plan will help you recover from a bad shot." He smiled and left. We haven't run into each other since.

The seventeenth reason golf is better than sex:
If you die in the middle of a round, it's not nearly so traumatic for your partner.

HOLE EIGHTEEN
THE INTERNATIONAL

Proper golf etiquette dictates that you remove your cap when shaking hands at the end of a round. You see the pros do it religiously. If they think it's the correct way to finish a round then that's good enough for me.

DECIDING WHICH HOLE TO USE to finish the round and Volume One was a challenge. There have been several exciting and fun finishes over the last twenty years. After thinking about it though the choice actually made itself. It was the round where one of my playing partners had a shot at par, Par-Man's ultimate goal.

"Let's play at the course at the apartments." Steve was in town doing some training for his new company and the accommodations that had been made for him included a couple of free rounds of golf at the Shawnee Golf and Country Club.

"Sure, it looks like a fun course. How about I stop by tomorrow about three and we'll give it a shot." Neither of us had ever played the course so it would be something new.

"Great, see you then."

That night I used Google Earth to get some idea of what to expect. Par-Man also went to their website. Preparation would help both of us have the best chance at reaching our goal.

When I looked at the course I knew there would be problems. While usually straight Par-Man was not particularly long off the tee. Shawnee Golf Club was a bit longer than courses I usually play. The greens were large and being a reasonably good putter that worked to my advantage. **[The largest green in the world is**

28000 square feet. It is the par 6 on the 5th hole at the Golf Club in Massachusetts.]

While I wasn't actually alone I was still a walk-on. Steve and I were assured that there was plenty of space and all we had to do was show up. True to their word the starter put us with two others and away we went. Turns out the other two members of our foursome were also visiting from out of town, actually way out of town.

"I'm E. J. and this is Steve."

They extended their hands but only one of them spoke. "So nice to be with you. I am called Louis and this is Jesus." (In this case I used real names. I'm pretty sure they won't mind, or even know.)

The accents were a give-away. They were from the southern part of the continent, Reynosa, Mexico to be exact. Being Mr. Observant, the custom clubs and near perfect swings told me these boys knew how to play the game. Yet again, Par-Man was spot on.

Jesus and Louis put on a damn clinic. Their drives were down the middle, approach shots always near the pin and smooth, real smooth, when putting. We had interesting conversations from one hole to the other. The conversations were a little stilted, but their English was much better than my Spanish.

For most golfers the difference between a three dollar ball and a one dollar ball is two dollars. These two visitors from our neighbor to the south would have known the difference. **[Jack Nicklaus said that golf is a game of misses. The guy that misses the best wins.]** Louis missed a couple of times but Jesus never did. By the time we got to the last hole there were two possible shots at the Par-Man goal, neither was the two gringos.

Jesus was two under as we stood at the eighteenth tee box, Louis was just one over. They were two of the nicest, friendliest men I ever had the pleasure of golfing with. They also had a good sense of humor. About the tenth hole Louis was taking a practice swing and stopped at the top of his take-away and looked at his hands. Jesus said, "You know stopping your backswing at the top and looking will tell you only two things. How many hands you have and which one is wearing the glove."

To make it even funnier he said it in Spanish and only he and Louis laughed. Steve and Par-Man stood there bewildered. "Oh, I am so sorry. How rude of me." When he told us what he said we laughed as well.

We learned some interesting things about golf in Mexico. There aren't very many courses that the average player can get on. Also, since it's a very hot climate and water is at a premium the greens and fairways are all small. They don't get to play on different grasses. He and Louis belong to a country club across the border in McAllen, Texas. They work for a company that has manufacturing in Reynosa but is headquartered in McAllen.

An American went to Scotland to play St. Andrew's; it had been a dream of his. To have his best chance at success he hired a caddy. Unfortunately nothing went right. The visitor to the country that invented this stupid game was learning that golf isn't and never will be a fair game. Finally he took his frustration out on his caddy. "You'll never help me get to one under on any of these holes."

"You've already been one under. You were under the tree, under the bush and now you are under the water."

"You are the worst caddy in the world."

Replying calmly the man carrying the clubs replied, "I doubt that, it would be too much of a coincidence."

At 400 hundred yards the eighteenth hole was fairly straight and void of sand or water. Par-Man and Steve, if we parred the hole would end up in the low eighties. Louis needed a birdie to get par but Jesus could get a double bogey and still end up at par for the eighteen. It seemed like a no brainer, especially after Jesus hit a screamer right down the middle.

There's a saying: The mind messes up more shots than the body. This was one of those cases. Jesus tried to be too precise and bladed the shot. It took off like a scalded cat, ran across the green and hid in the rough on the far side.

I don't know for sure what he said but Jesus let loose with a blast. If cursing had any effect on the trajectory of a golf ball Jesus' last shot would be just inches from the cup. Since it was all in Spanish the only one that would care was Louis. Returning to the cart he kicked his golf bag. That seemed to calm him down. **[Up until 1890 the caddies carried the clubs using a strap tied around each club. After that the golf bag came into vogue.]**

I was long on my approach so both Par-Man and Jesus were on the back of the green looking at essentially the same shot. Jesus was out but he would have to practically stand on my ball to make his shot.

"Is it going to go left or right? I see it's downhill, but boy that looks like it could break either way." It was a confusing read.

"I see what you mean. I also am unsure." As he approached his ball it was clear that he was concerned.

"I don't want you to stand awkwardly because of my ball so I will hit first and get out of your way."

Looking at me suspiciously he nodded his agreement. Chipping up we were both a little surprised to see the ball break left and then right. Par-Man ended up twelve feet away.

Looking back at Jesus it was time for Par-Man to make sure he relaxed. "I don't know if it's true in Mexico but the difference here between golf and government is in golf you can't improve your lie."

Looking up he seemed perplexed. Then he started laughing. Then he laughed even harder. "In my language a lie, like an untruth and a lie, as in where the ball rests, are two different words. When I translated your words in my head they made no sense. Then I translated them back and I understood."

That about sums it up. Jesus chipped on and one putted. The par put him two under. Four men from all over North America played a game that required no explanation. We all understood the rules, protocols and etiquette. Ain't golf a wonderful sport?

The eighteenth reason that golf is better than sex:
It's perfectly all right to stop in the middle and have a hot dog and beer.

HOLE NINETEEN

Proper golf etiquette is for the winner to offer to buy the first round. It's all right to pay immediately, that way you don't get stuck with a huge tab.

FINALLY, EVERYONE CAN RELAX. Sit with your friends, have a beer, swap stories and trade words of wisdom. You know things like: In golf close enough or good enough is never close enough or good enough. Or, if you grip a knife and fork as poorly as you do a golf club, you're going to starve to death. Then there's my personal favorite, if you are going to throw a club, it is important to throw it ahead of you, down the fairway, so you don't have to waste energy going back to pick it up.

In general golfers are a philosophical bunch. We know that if you don't mind playing golf in the rain, snow or even during a hurricane then your life is in serious trouble. We ponder the mysteries of the fairways. For instance, why is it harder to hit a ball over the water than sand? Or why you have to swing easy to hit hard.

We also believe in the cosmic nature of things. If you get a birdie then someone has to get a couple of bogies to bring the universe back into balance. If you hit your ball in the fairway and then can't find it, it's because it fell into a divot that is connected to a vaporizing wormhole. There is a logical explanation for everything except how a two foot putt can break eight inches to the left.

Besides being fodder for the philosophical side of human nature golf is a great educational tool. I know a man who is the president of a major company and insists on playing eighteen holes with anyone being considered for a management position. There is no doubt that one afternoon of golf will teach you more about a person than 18 years of dealing with them across a desk. It's the essence of the game.

Once the frivolity winds down and it is time to head home to the missus remember what Dean Martin used to say, "Don't drink and drive, hell don't even putt." Every golfer out there knows that after that last putt drops home the clock starts ticking. Each golfer now starts keeping track of how long until the next round, the next chance at perfection and the next possibility of being teamed with Par-Man.

The nineteenth reason golf is better than sex:
It's perfectly acceptable to sit in the bar when you are done and brag to your buddies about your success.

www.ingramcontent.com/pod-product-compliance
Lightning Source LLC
Chambersburg PA
CBHW070853050426
42453CB00012B/2181